Advance Praise for
A Brush with Darkness

"Lisa tells her unique, heart-touching story with the same beautiful, vivid, and colorful style that she paints. She leaves us wondering which is the real world: the one outside or the one inside ourselves."

—MARISA DARNEL, associate editor of
Artist Interviews Magazine

"This book is powerful enough to dispel most of the myths, negative images, and stereotypes that people have held against those with disabilities in general, and blindness in particular, for centuries. Ms. Fittipaldi is both an outstanding writer and an artist who happens to have a disability. I recommend this book to anyone who enjoys a great story that is written well."

—GEORGE A. COVINGTON, legally blind photographer and
former Special Assistant for Disability Policy
to Vice President Dan Quayle

"Lisa Fittipaldi's book, *A Brush with Darkness,* is a very unusual work. It tells the story of a very rare human achievement, overcoming the limitations of blindness and creating painted images characterized by a great precision of outline. In her direct, intuitive way, Lisa Fittipaldi also touches on some of the great problems with which painters have been concerned for centuries. She shows, in an altogether surprising way, that image-making in painting is, first of all, a matter of the mind, no less, and in some rare cases even more, than of the seeing eye."

—MOSHE BARASCH, art historian and author of
Blindness: The History of a Mental Image in Western Thought

"Blindness in any degree is horrifying enough; though often incurable, it is not without edifying realizations. *A Brush with Darkness* is Lisa Fittipaldi's slog through despair and helplessness, a trek toward acceptance of the compromised self and, ultimately, a triumphal strut over whine and circumstance."

—CÉSAR A. MARTÍNEZ, artist

A BRUSH WITH DARKNESS

Learning to *Paint* After Losing My Sight

LISA FITTIPALDI

Andrews McMeel
Publishing

Kansas City

04 05 06 07 08 TWP 10 9 8 7 6 5 4 3 2 1

Library of Congress Cataloging-in-Publication Data

Fittipaldi, Lisa.
    A brush with darkness : learning to paint after losing my sight / Lisa Fittipaldi.
        p. cm.
     ISBN 0-7407-4693-6
     1. Fittipaldi, Lisa. 2. Blind women—Texas—Biography. 3. Blind artists—Texas—Biography. 4. Blindness—Texas—Case studies. 5. Art and vision disorders. I. Title.

HV1792.F57A3 2004
305.9'081'092—dc22
[B]

2004048055

Book design by Pete Lippincott

ATTENTION: SCHOOLS AND BUSINESSES

Andrews McMeel books are available at quantity discounts with bulk purchase for educational, business, or sales promotional use. For information, please write to: Special Sales Department, Andrews McMeel Publishing, 4520 Main Street, Kansas City, Missouri 64111.

To Al,

with thanks for that first watercolor set
and all that followed

TABLE OF CONTENTS

Acknowledgments viii

Introduction ix

Part I Retreat 1

   CHAPTER ONE   Darkness Falls 3

   CHAPTER TWO   Vanishing Point 20

   CHAPTER THREE   Shadow Play 39

Part II Regroup 59

   CHAPTER FOUR   First Light 61

   CHAPTER FIVE   Walking in Space 81

   CHAPTER SIX   Painting in the Dark 97

   CHAPTER SEVEN   On the Road 117

   CHAPTER EIGHT   The Blind Artist 130

Part III Return 153

   CHAPTER NINE   Course Correction 155

   CHAPTER TEN   An Artist Who Happens to
                        Be Blind 178

   CHAPTER ELEVEN   The Mind's Eye, the Heart's Ease . . 201

ACKNOWLEDGMENTS

Bringing this book to publication involved the dedicated effort and support of many people. I would especially like to express my deep appreciation and thanks to a few of them:

Agent Jeff Kleinman believed in this project and persisted in finding the right publisher.

Editor Jean Lucas, marketing director Rebecca Murray, and the lovely staff at Andrews McMeel have been a pleasure to work with.

Art dealer extraordinaire Jason Siegel critiqued my self-portrait and always encourages me to keep painting.

Laura (Lulu) Torbet's collaboration on this book helped to organize, shape, and polish the thoughts I was hesitant to put down on paper. She asked the right questions, understood the answers, and has become a friend. Without her guiding hand, this project would not have come to fruition. The process was so smooth that our months of working together seemed like minutes. A special thanks to Lulu for my banana socks.

And finally to Al Fittipaldi, who challenged me to paint, and who in every way has supported my career as an artist. He read every word of every draft of this book out loud to me and uncomplainingly makes me coffee in the wee hours of the night. He is my guiding light.

INTRODUCTION

When my vision began to fail, I was married, with a well-paying job as a financial analyst at a hospital in Austin, Texas. We had a comfortable suburban home, social friends, and the freedom to dream about our next car, or vacation, or swimming pool. My life might have continued like this to the end of my days. But I was lucky. I lost my sight and was diagnosed with a degenerative chronic disease that forecasts an untimely death.

"The mass of men," Thoreau said, "lead lives of quiet desperation." Though I did not recognize it, I was one of them. A comfortable life free of crisis or complications is not much of a goal, but given my painful past, I dared not dream of anything more. I dealt with my difficult childhood through escape and denial, and had long ago walled off my emotions.

In the early days of my vision loss, someone reminded me that the Chinese pictogram for *crisis* shares the same root as the one for *opportunity*. This made no sense at all to me. I wanted my old life back. With few inner resources to fall back on, I lived for a very long time in a fugue of anger-fueled fear and depression. My stubborn refusal to accept my fate and adapt to it almost did me in.

Today, I am considered the world's only profoundly blind realist painter. My work is shown and sold worldwide. I direct a foundation that provides adaptive computer technology for children who are blind or have vision and hearing impairments, which enables them to mainstream in public schools. My husband, Al, and I run a bed-and-breakfast in San Antonio, Texas. Blindness has, against all logic, given me great gifts. How I wish I could have acquired clarity of vision without losing my sight.

I've come to believe that people succeed *because* of crisis, not in spite of it. Few of us voluntarily make the changes necessary to live our lives to the fullest. It's too scary to break out of our comfort zone, to move from the predictable into the unknown. What if we fail? What if our life takes a turn for the worse? What if those we depend on abandon us? There is no way to prepare for blindness—or cancer, or the death of a loved one, or having your house burn down. One can only be prepared to accept and adapt to life as it happens, to be able to handle life's inevitable difficulties in a graceful and productive way. Probably like everyone who has surmounted obstacles they now view as gifts, I want to encourage others to rise to whatever challenges life offers. In the process of making lemonade from lemons, we ourselves are transformed.

Blindness is pretty much everyone's worst nightmare. Most of us have tried to imagine it. I am here to tell you that, yes, it is unimaginable. There are still days when I'm so exhausted and discouraged that I wonder if I'm going to make it. I want to convey firsthand the terror of limitless empty spaces, the seemingly innocuous danger of a spoon left on the floor, the insurmountable obstacle of finding that something has not been put back in its place. I want to describe the minute-by-minute multisensory attention needed to get through every waking hour of every day. I want to report what it's like to be a disabled person in the world of the "whole." I also want to tell you that I wouldn't trade my life today to have my sight back.

A Brush with Darkness is about how I made my way back into the world, one breath and one day at a time, to become an artist. There is nothing magical about my ability to paint. I am not channeling Degas. From the beginning, learning to paint was a practical, survival-oriented quest to find my way in the dark void that surrounded me. It required every ounce of my attention, intellect, and spirit. This book recounts the obstacle-strewn course of my odyssey, from the day in 1993 when the world first disappeared to today, when I have recaptured it. It is not always an uplifting story. Big chunks of *A Brush with Darkness* unfold as I stumble, weary and depressed, terrified and angry, through a dark landscape. I am not a brave and glamorous storybook heroine. My guess is that you will find me extremely annoying at times, as did everyone around me in the early days.

I wrote this book for both sighted and blind readers, in the hope that my story can help others on their journey. I want to share what I have learned about art and perception. But I also wrote this book for myself. Only now, these many years later, have I found the bedrock trust and equanimity to exorcise my dark demons in public.

PART I

RETREAT

CHAPTER ONE

DARKNESS FALLS

Art is the triumph over chaos.

—JOHN CHEEVER

ON A CRISP CLOUDLESS MORNING in March 1993, the world disappeared before my eyes as I drove to work at an Austin hospital. For the briefest second, blackness swallowed the tractor-trailer in front of me. So quickly and quietly did the moment pass that I chalked it up to a black hole, a random glitch in the universal order that had nothing to do with me. I continued on my commute to work, stopping along the way to pick up my usual cup of coffee.

Two weeks later, in the crush of Monday morning rush hour, it happened again. This time the incident was so vivid in its slow-motion detail that I couldn't disown it. To this day, the memory chills me to the bone.

The stretch of I-35 between Airport Boulevard and Manor Road is notoriously brutal to navigate. Armadas of giant trucks whiz by on their way to Mexico. Office-bound cars jostle to shave seconds off their time, darting in and out of lanes. Oil and heated tar slick the road surface. The din of horns, sirens, and wheels on the upper deck punctuate the staccato flashes of light bouncing off chrome and mirrors. That day, bright shafts of natural light pierced the shadows, confusing the curves of the interstate as the sun rose hot and heavy on another Texas day..

I had descended to the treacherous tangle of off-ramps at Exit 235A, where the lanes narrow and the road shoulder is almost nonexistent. On Monday mornings I was always extra cautious, turning off the radio and slowing down on this last dangerous stretch before my exit. This particular morning I was unexplainably tired, as though the lethargy of the weekend had stolen my reflexive edge.

Suddenly I was stunned by the high-pitched squeal of brakes from the pickup truck on my left. Horns blared from the rear and right, car tires screamed as they swerved to avoid an impact. Turning to see where the noises were coming from, I was dumbstruck. My world had again turned black. The steering wheel and dashboard had disappeared. The huge tractor-trailer in front me, the bright blue pickup, the sea of bumper-to-bumper traffic—all vanished. A moment ago, the passenger door of my Honda was inches from the concrete wall of the lower deck. Now, nothing. I leaned on the horn to warn others, feeling the pins and needles of the adrenaline rush as I pulled to the right and hit the brakes, bracing myself for the inevitable clash of steel on steel, for the smell of diesel mixed with gasoline.

But it was suddenly quiet. *Maybe I'm home in bed. I'm simply having a bad dream.* I became aware of my surroundings in slow stages, sensing the urgent flow of traffic careening silently around my stalled car hugging the ramp wall. *I'm having a stroke. A heart attack. I'm going to die!* I sat there paralyzed in panicked confusion, my heart pounding hard enough to punch a hole in my chest. My palms slipped wildly on the steering wheel as I dissolved into a sweaty puddle on the cloth seat.

Insistent sounds began to pierce my trance, and the world slid crookedly back into focus. I struggled to recover, my front bumper enveloped by the belching diesel of a tractor-trailer, the passenger-side mirror crushed from a nearly disastrous brush with the pickup, cars screeching around me. *Calm down. Move.* Gulping for breath, I inched myself off the expressway.

I escaped the whirlwind to find myself parked in the empty field behind the University of Texas stadium. The moment I shut the engine off I began trembling in earnest. My hands and feet were stone cold. *What had happened back there? Was I having a nervous breakdown? A migraine? Was almost being in an auto accident so unnerving that I just fell apart?* Unable, and unwilling, to think about what had occurred, I put my head on the steering wheel and, feeling the icy grip of panic loosen, I sobbed.

Fumbling with my car phone, I called my husband, Al, at work, struggling to explain the bizarre circumstances of the last few minutes. "Stay put. I'll be there as soon as I can," he commanded. I dialed work, evasively reporting that I'd been in an automobile accident. How else to explain that one moment the world was clear and bright, that my brain and eyes were functioning in tandem, and the next instant everything had vanished? I needed a reasonable explanation as much as anyone.

I checked myself over for blood, broken bones, bruises, *any* evidence that something traumatic had happened. Nothing. No apparent clues to this brush with darkness. But even the desire to deny my experience could not entirely block out the fact that something awful had transpired. I dialed my physician to schedule an appointment later that day, telling his nurse that I had been involved in an accident, avoiding the murky details. I certainly did not want the office staff to think I was losing my grip. Already I was operating in my all too familiar "what will people think?" mode.

With the motor off, the hum of the freeway offered a cocoon of white noise. I locked the car door to await Al and the return to normalcy. An hour later I awoke from a drugged sleep to an insistent tapping on the driver's window. The sudden blackout of the world made me afraid to open my eyes. But when I finally mustered the courage to sneak a peek, there were Al and his friend Tom to rescue me. My vision was normal. *Thank heaven.* I stepped out of the car on jellyfish legs and shuffled to the passenger's side for the drive home. Tom followed close behind, assuming that the Honda was having some sort of mechanical difficulty.

By the time we returned safely to our home in Georgetown, the whole episode seemed like a distant dream. I was just fine, thank you, emotionally and physically. Actually, I was feeling stupid for having had such a melodramatic reaction to what now seemed like a minor event. I canceled the appointment with the doctor, not wanting to seem hysterical. Al went along with my nonchalance, seconding my notion that there was probably nothing wrong. Perhaps I was just overtired and had nodded off at the wheel for a moment, he conjectured. "At least you weren't hurt."

We settled down a bit now that the initial excitement was over, and had a bite of lunch. But the fragile veneer of my denial was repeatedly punctured by reality attacks. I remembered the blackness. From one moment to the next I vacillated between feeling that everything was fine and fearing that the worst was yet to come. Al chided me for being a pessimist, for wanting to believe that this incident was a serious omen, for feeling so shattered and anxious when no apparent harm had been done. Maybe Al was right; I was overreacting. Then the niggling thought crept in: *Of course, I didn't tell him about the first incident.* My little secret, the first of many.

Thus began my slippery, scary slide into darkness. Unconsciously I knew something that my rational mind wasn't yet able to admit, and my free-floating dread would simply not go away. For the next several days, as a precaution, I took the city commuter-van service to work. But when a week passed with no further episodes, I began to believe, like Al, that my blackouts were just isolated, nonrelated incidents. Stress, maybe. Or, as I'd first thought, merely a momentary wrinkle in time.

That weekend I was in the garden fighting a losing battle with the fire ants when an assortment of "bugs" floated in front of my eyes. Roaches and spiders sprang up everywhere I looked. I tried brushing them away, but eventually I realized that they were not really "out there." *I must be tired,* I told myself. *I haven't eaten anything since breakfast. I'll get a glass of juice.* As I was reaching into the refrigerator, darkness fell like a curtain over my world, and my knees buckled. I was overcome with a terrifying certainty that these episodes were not going to go away. Something was very wrong with my vision, and it was getting worse.

Thus began months of living in parallel and noncommunicating universes. In one universe, my vision fluctuated wildly, moments of clarity interspersed with dead blackness and dark amoebic shapes randomly blocking my field of vision. In this universe, I dealt with my failing vision. I went from doctor to doctor, test to test, and from abject terror to wild hope, desperate to solve a problem that defied a clear diagnosis. The parallel universe was the one in which I pretended, to myself and everyone else, with every ounce of determination I could muster, that I could still see, could still do my job, and that my eyes would be fine. In this world denial and depression blanketed the fear.

It was quite a dance. On the Monday morning following the blackout at Exit 235A, I drove to work, having convinced myself that seeing bugs before my eyes would warn me of vision blackouts. I notified my boss that I had a doctor's appointment as a follow-up to my accident the week before and would be leaving early. That afternoon I told my family practitioner an only slightly sanitized version of what had occurred.

"I've been noticing a fleeting loss of vision," I reported.

"It's stress," he quickly concluded, having gathered no further evidence beyond my less than frank report and the usual blood pressure and temperature measurements. Would I like to take something for my nerves? He asked no further questions about my symptoms, and I wasn't about to press for a more dire diagnosis. I was all too happy to make him my first ally in denial. Declining the medication, I went home elated that my problem was "just stress."

Two days later I spent a hair-raising hour in sporadic darkness coupled with diamondlike patterns flashing before my eyes. These episodes of bugs, flashes, and floaters began to occur ever more frequently, without warning, at any time of the day or night. They would typically last for a few seconds, and seemed totally unrelated to any specific stress or activity. Admitting to myself—but to no one else—that I was a hazard on the road, I again signed up for the commuter van.

In a relentless cascade, the episodes of blindness escalated in their frequency, duration, and ferocity. One day at work, I had a headache and static wavy patterns appeared in my field of vision. This time the apparitions did not go away in a few seconds or minutes, and over the course of several hours a diaphanous curtain formed over my eyes. Other symptoms came and went, from chest pain and numbness in my hands and face to vertigo and double vision.

Now I was really scared. I called my primary care physician's office again and explained my problem to the nurse, who then called an internal medicine specialist. I wanted this problem fixed *now,* but my HMO offered an appointment for the following month. Certain that I had a brain tumor, that cells were mutating and ready to explode, I pleaded for an earlier appointment, but the earliest available time slot was three days away. Three days of waking nightmares, convinced that my brain was disintegrating and neurosurgery was next. Three days without food or sleep, in a suffocating agony of darkness interspersed with wild hope after each moment of clear vision. Three days in which I went to work and pretended I could function.

Finally, the appointment came. A battery of tests was ordered: blood tests for cancer, diabetes, and thyroid problems, EKGs, sonograms, a test to rule out an aneurysm, and an MRI to eliminate the possibility of heart disease and stroke. I was referred to a neurologist and an ophthalmologist; these referrals led to more tests and diagnostic exams. When the results were inconclusive, I was moved on to another specialist. Every test raised new speculations. Perhaps I had a detached retina. Perhaps corneal distortion, maybe damage to the iris or lens or sclera? They suspected a condition called papillitis, which sometimes manifests as a transient blind spot in the eye. Nothing seemed to fit my symptoms. So I was passed on to a hematologist, followed by a rheumatologist and a cardiologist. Appointments with an allergist, a dermatologist, an immunologist, and an endocrinologist followed. Test upon test and more tests. I was running out of body parts and systems to examine. *See, it's only stress.*

Three months passed. It was now the end of May and the episodes of floaters, bugs, and visual distortion persisted. Yet every test came up negative or inconclusive. All the doctors agreed that my intermittent, transient episodes of vision loss were a serious problem, but they could not figure out why.

Every negative result gave me hope. Before the incident on I-35, I had ignored some low-level vision problems as the onset of menopause. Could menopause still explain my symptoms? *Maybe there is nothing really wrong with me.*

The frustrated specialists concluded that what I needed was a psychiatrist and perhaps, just to be safe, another ophthalmologist and more eye examinations. Still, nothing seemed to fit my symptoms, so it was on to the next tier of ophthalmologists, neurologists, and rheumatologists. By this time I had visited nearly a hundred doctors and had had every imaginable mainstream medical test. Every week was a juggling act of tests, medical forms, and appointments, sandwiched between my home life and the continuing charade at work, all for an issue I was still pretending would go away. The bills were mounting up, as was my terror, though anger and frustration helped keep my fears at bay. I was losing my patience. I had to remind myself, however, that a part of me was avoiding telling the whole truth about my situation, on the off chance that ignorance might just possibly turn out to be bliss.

The psychiatrist recommended by the HMO felt that I would be better served if I connected with the gurus at Houston's Cullen Eye Institute. By this time, my periods of vision loss were totally unpredictable. The doctors were beginning to believe that I was dealing with late-onset multiple sclerosis or, just possibly, an autoimmune disease. They wanted to run more esoteric tests, but the HMO protested that a forty-nine-year-old woman like me did not fit the "profile" of an older white male prone to the type of autoimmune disease the doctors now suspected. They refused to approve any more tests without a definitive diagnosis.

We were in limbo. The doctors felt they could not risk treating me until my disease had a proper label. A misdiagnosis and improper treatment might make my problem worse and could even lead to my death. So Al and I waited. I used up all of my vacation time from work while I was tested again and sent off to more specialists. We wrote more letters to the HMO, pleading for tests that would permit a proper diagnosis and treatment. The frustrations mounted. As my fears accumulated, my attitude toward the medical profession became increasingly cynical. I was a walking bundle of nerves and irritability. An innocuous remark or a minor inconvenience would provoke me into explosive outbursts of temper. More evidence that my problem might be merely menopause.

In good faith I tried the well-meaning recommendations of friends for alternative treatments to alleviate my symptoms and tension: acupuncture, megavitamins, massage, aromatherapy, herbal remedies. Nothing seemed to offer much relief. Finally I decided that enough was enough. I was done with the entire business. No conclusive results, no consistent impediments, and therefore no problem. *Nothing serious.* I resented having spent so much money for nothing, and I chastised myself for being unable to cope with this minor problem. Having kept a firm hold on my actions and emotions all my life, I was upset with myself for feeling so out of control.

It was quite a challenge to maintain my stubborn denial at this stage. One minute I'd be able to read and scan and function, and the next moment, my eyes would short out, for no discernible reason. I might be in the middle of a high-stress task or simply relaxing, doing nothing in particular, when the lights would dim and fade. I would cross a room, scanning for details and points of reference, preplanning my movement. Another blink and I'd open my eyes to darkness. Days would go by and my vision would hold true. No black spots, no bugs or flashes of light. Then, without warning, the internal computer chip would unseat and my eyes would not function. I would endure whole minutes and sometimes hours, heart-pounding hours, in darkness, minutes and hours praying only to blink and see.

It seemed to me that the loss of my sight was not the worst part. The anguish and frustration of not knowing when my sight would disappear—or if it would reappear—was unbearable. Like the eyes of a person with glaucoma or macular degeneration, mine appeared normal, but the interactions between my eyes, brain, and optic nerves were out of sync. My mind started playing tricks. I began to anticipate on a deep intellectual level what I *should* be seeing. But increasingly I found that the images I conjured existed only in my mind. I began to doubt my previsualizations of the world. *Is that really a measuring cup? Is he wearing a striped tie? Are those light reflections on the pond?* I would find myself staring at an object, unable to verify whether it was real or imagined. I would then wait for someone to confirm that the object was really what I thought I was seeing.

We are visual creatures. The world comes to us through our eyes. About 70 percent of our decision-making ability is based on sight. Not just the knowledge that a car is approaching, or a chair is blocking our way, or there's a stone in our path. It's the eye that decides, "Yes, I'll take that pink sweater" or "That custard pie makes my mouth water." We take in information about people on sight, and make snap decisions about whether to approach or retreat. We evaluate the weather and plot the steps to our destination. We are used to seeing things "with our own eyes."

When we lose our sight, we lose our primary means of connection to the world. Without sight, the brain is like a camera that has run out of film. The mind craves sustenance. Deprived of its main source of nourishment, it panics. No longer receiving a constant stream of information, the brain atrophies from lack of stimulation. Fantasy and unverifiable distortions can easily take hold. Only diligent intellectual stimulation and multi-sensory replacement feeding keep the brain alive and well.

I could feel myself sinking into emotional darkness as my eyes failed. My refusal to acknowledge the severity of my problem was taking its toll, as was the lack of a diagnosis. I was lost in a maze. I knew there must be an exit, but every time I turned a corner, I encountered another dead end. As my confusion increased, my ability to cope diminished. Unlike people with progressive eye diseases, I could not count on a slow and consistent decline in vision or the concomitant time available to adapt. My vision loss was unpredictable, and speeding rapidly to an unknown end. What was I to do, except to try to keep up the pretense that I still had perfect sight?

Denial and deception were strategies I knew well from childhood. Unwanted by parents whose desire for children was negligible, and whose definition of the ideal daughter I didn't come close to matching, I was often relieved when I had to spend time in the hospital to treat my severe asthma and eczema. In truth, I preferred the hospital, where I felt cherished and praised, to life at home.

My social-climbing mother had wanted a popular, pretty daughter. Instead she got me, a short, dark, pudgy girl too smart for her own good. So she traded me for my pretty, pliable cousin Laurie, sending me off to live with an aunt and uncle, or with my grandparents. My grandparents were quite a pair. My mean-spirited grandmother was happy only when others were not. My mild-mannered grandfather was a perpetual optimist. His soothing presence was a balm to my wounded spirit. They seemed to love me, but how could I trust that they weren't simply meeting an obligation?

My mother took pleasure in tormenting me. Her cruelty taught me that self-reliance and emotional withdrawal were the most effective survival skills. I would escape the harsh world of my mother's rages with a novel or a biography until the storm had passed. Left alone for long stretches, I learned to revel in my own silent world. I would fall asleep solving complex algebra equations or brainteasers from the daily paper. Stung by criticism, I'd work harder to excel at school. My father was kinder than my mother. He at least made it clear to me that his neglect wasn't personal. His only interest in life was his business. When my parents did take an interest in my life, their cruelty was so devastating that I prayed daily for their indifference and neglect.

But this was a crisis of a higher magnitude; it demanded my cunning and vigilance in full measure. It was literally unthinkable that I might permanently lose my sight. There was no way to prove my worth that didn't require vision, and no effective escape stratagems. I could not imagine a way to go on, except to try to live as I always had, as best I could. There was only deception, of myself and others. If I let down my defenses, if I once slipped up in my efforts and vigilance, I would be engulfed in a flood of terrible and irreversible change. I would again be an unwanted outsider. I couldn't bear it.

Keeping up appearances seems a hilarious strategy for someone who can't see, but I tried my best. I rearranged my schedule to work a four-day week, in order to pursue my stealthy medical quest. To keep others from detecting my deficits, I would arrive on the early commuter van and fumble my way through the hospital and into my office. Clumsily groping my way along the walls, feeling for the backs of chairs and counting rows of desks, I'd spend tense minutes scurrying around to recover pens and folders that I'd sent flying en route. When I ended up in the wrong place, I started over, backtracking and recounting until I identified my own office, desk, and seat. There I stayed for the duration of the day. It was beyond my feeble navigation abilities to locate the bathroom, cafeteria, or coffee machine.

Pulling off a plausible imitation of working was even harder than getting there. I used every imaginable trick to give the appearance that I knew what I was doing. At the sound of foot-steps, I would snap straight in my chair and type gibberish into my computer.

"Oh, I've decided that's not important right now," I'd claim when someone wanted my quarterly projections. Or "I've got to finish this analysis. Would you read this over for me and report back tomorrow?"

Riding home, someone on the van would let me know when to notify the driver of my stop. Then I would wait at the Park-n-Ride until Al came to retrieve me. This last hour of the working day was the most frightening. I would alight from the van to the deserted parking lot, afraid to move from the spot. Everything and everyone around me was a mystery and a threat. The chittering birds and breeze-blown trees, the drone of the cicadas, the whoosh of rush-hour traffic, and the steam rising from the cooling asphalt as evening fell all reinforced my feelings of vulnerability. *What if Al doesn't come?* I was stranded in my pool of darkness, at the mercy of my fickle vision and my stubbornness. *I have to stop this charade. I can't keep it up anymore.* Just when I was sure I couldn't stand it another minute—*I have to get a cane. I'm going to learn Braille*—Al would pull up and help me into the car, into the safety zone.

Now Al took over, supplying me with food, directions, supplies, news, and solace. Over dinner, he read my mail and memos out loud. I'd dictate my correspondence and have him add up my figures. This was not efficient, and it was exhausting, but I could think of no alternative. Afterward, we'd lay out my clothes and get me showered. Only sheer exhaustion allowed me a night's sleep. Thus did the subterfuge continue. Al played along . . . for a while.

Weekends offered not only needed recuperation time but the opportunity to enlist Al's services to catch up on work demands. I prayed for the increasingly rare interludes of clear vision that allowed me to write reports, organize my clothes for the week, and reorient myself to my fast-fading world. I gave up trying to arrange my hair or apply makeup. I was constantly anxious, ever vigilant of my diminishing vestiges of power or control. All I could do was try my best to hang on.

Every morning I woke up wondering if I would see my face in the mirror. Imagine going to your closet to dress, laying your clothes out onto the bed, organizing each item in the precise order it will be put on, just in case, in the middle of dressing, the objects you have laid out start fading to blackness. Or imagine yourself looking in the mirror to put on mascara. You blink, and suddenly you can't apply mascara to your other eye because once again you are in the dark. At times my vision would seem stable, and I was all too willing to take the bait. *See, I'm fine.* I'd rush out to cut the lawn with the riding mower, only to find myself bobbing helplessly in a sea of darkness from which there was no exit. I was playing an insidious mind game of my own device.

I could not—perhaps I dared not—explain to myself, my husband, or the doctors precisely what was happening, and how often. Sometimes what I experienced was like the snow and static of the cable-TV reception going haywire. At other times the wandering amoebic shapes or the crawly bugs reappeared. Or there'd be patterns and flashes of light. I would shake my head or take a deep breath, and the imagery of the world would rematerialize in perfect order. Other times I would do nothing at all and my vision would return. There was apparently no method to this madness. The frustration of not knowing when I would see felt worse than the fear of losing my sight. Without a specific diagnosis, the constant fluctuations in vision, which I'd managed through sheer will to view as an inconvenience, were ruling my life. Every action, every thought had to be planned around the probability that in the next second, moment, hour, or day, I would not be able to see. The calculations involved in simply walking downstairs to get something to eat were exhausting.

No matter how hard I worked, no matter how I distracted myself, I spent a lot of time obsessing. If I stand up, will the floaters come back? Is there something I could eat that would help? Do my coworkers believe I can still see? Will this be the day that the doctors make a diagnosis? Did I forget to bring my files home? What is this new tingling in my arm? Will this fluctuation in my vision go away, or is there more anguish and hardship in store? My hard-won denial was weakening, as was my self-control. Hope was fading.

By the end of August I would have welcomed a lethal brain tumor—anything to free me from the hell of uncertainty. I would have preferred to be told I was going to die in the next few weeks. Then I could just stop. The terrible strain would be over, and I could let go to the inevitable. At least I would know for certain what was wrong with me, and I could live accordingly. A resolution of this situation, whatever form it might take, was eminent in my mind.

September arrived in a blaze of heat and a blast of cold. I was scheduled to see another series of specialists for yet another battery of tests. The prognosis did not look good. The consensus was that my eyesight was rapidly failing. *Duh*. In March I had been 20/20. Now my vision was less than 20/200, corrected, in both eyes. I had developed periorbital cataracts, an inflammation and swelling of the lens of the eye. My corneas were deteriorating at an alarming rate. As to why, the doctors remained baffled.

In an attempt to slow the ulceration and degeneration of my corneas, I had been fitted with specially designed contact lenses. I was on my eighth pair in five months, each in escalating strength. My asthma, dormant for over twenty years, was kicking up with a vengeance. Symptoms of various unrelated diseases popped up to complicated matters, but still the doctors could not put a medical label on my problems. Medication I'd previously used for my asthma precipitated a 911 call, an emergency room visit, and several days in the ICU on respirator support.

Everyone concerned was now officially terrified. Al threatened to sue the hospital and HMO, and demanded that yet another specialist oversee my case. This is the point when we realized that my care was suffering in the hands of an organization that was concerned only with the bottom line. Al felt we had wasted a significant amount of time and money for less than adequate care. We switched from an HMO to a PPO medical plan.

Enrolling in a PPO didn't change my status, but it did improve the quality of my care. Now I was referred to top-level specialists, who were all but certain that I had some sort of rare autoimmune disease. The day finally came when, even without a firm diagnosis, my new ophthalmologist declared me legally blind. The label was optic neuritis (caused by the lack of sufficient blood supply to my optic nerve). Further investigations would determine if my problems were restricted to the eye.

In a matter of six months, my life had changed irrevocably. Al and I sat in the ophthalmologist's consulting room and heard the verdict: "I am declaring you legally blind and I am referring you to the Texas Commission for the Blind for rehabilitation."

Even though the truth was self-evident, we were stunned. The doctors were so clinical and matter-of-fact. "How many patients are declared legally blind each year?" Al asked. "Where do we go to fix this problem? Will her vision continue to deteriorate? What do we do now?" He wanted to know everything.

Al had hundreds of questions, and I had none. I knew perfectly well that I was blind. I knew perfectly well that my body was undergoing extreme changes, and I suspected that my dwindling vision was just the most obvious manifestation of these changes. But emotionally I was not ready to accept the label or the change. I was still unwilling to do the only thing that could save me now—adapt to my new life.

I began to weep. I dimly heard Al's voice droning, over and over, that this day had been coming for six months. "The label does not change anything," he kept repeating. "Your life has been leading to this moment since that day in March." Now all that concerned him was a plan to help me retain what sight remained. No one could foresee that one day I would see nothing but snow and shadows. How could they say I was legally blind when there were still times when I could see? Surely this was not truly blindness.

CHAPTER TWO

VANISHING POINT

We move between two darknesses.

—E. M. FORSTER

SO NOW I WAS "LEGALLY" BLIND, but I had no conception of what that label meant. I knew I could no longer see the large green informational signs on the highway or, for that matter, my big toe. The E at the top of the ophthalmologist's chart had disappeared months ago. Technically, legal blindness is defined as "visual acuity of 20/200 or less in the better eye, even with corrective lenses." For most people, it's a major impediment. You can't drive, you can't read even large-print books, and you are taking chances with your life when you try to cross the street unaided.

But I had my own definition. For me blindness simply meant that my pretense of leading a normal life was getting harder to pull off. Now I was a *legally* blind person pretending to see. No one could deal with my insistent denial. Everything I did was geared not toward rehabilitation but toward deception. Where before I would patiently wait for moments of visual clarity before finishing a task, now I just forged ahead, working in periods of intermittent darkness and light regardless of the consequences. These consequences ranged from the innocuous and hilarious—calling people by the wrong name, drinking salad dressing—to the dire—getting sideswiped by cars or nearly burning down the house.

Soon the periods of compensatory sight had all but disappeared, and I was left in a world of permanent visual distortion. My eyes were bombarded with intense light flashes, amoebalike floaters, a multitude of imaginary critters. The optical disintegration was so severe that I would mistake a log for an animal, and vice versa. I could not judge the size or distance of objects. I could no longer process my environment in anything close to real-time speed. Every change in light, every change in color, every noise left me startled and unnerved. Every sound made me feel vulnerable, anxious, and alone.

Riding in a car was terrifying. Colors and lights would flash in the periphery of my vision one moment; then darkness would engulf me. The sensation of speed, the stopping and starting and banking on the curves, the sound of the wind and the noise of the tires on the road, coupled with the ever-changing patterns of light, were all amplified by my inability to anticipate what was happening. Once I had loved the adrenaline rush of roller coasters. But the butterflies in my stomach no longer produced the exhilarating sensation of an amusement park ride. Now the butterflies never went away. Every time I left my house, fear of the unknowable world produced a full-bore adrenaline rush that didn't subside until I returned safely home. I had stepped into a Twilight Zone where Rod Serling's ominous voice intoned that I had entered another dimension, a timeless, sightless dimension outside the realm of normal human experience that would never, ever be interrupted for a commercial break.

Knowing that there was no exit from my predicament terrified me as much as the suffocating darkness. I could think of no acceptable way to solve my problem. How was I to go on, except to deny the seriousness of my situation? As long as I can keep up appearances, I rationalized, I can survive. I was convinced that if I accepted my blindness, my life would be over.

Throughout my life, I had done everything possible to maintain control of my fate. Other than denial, my defense mechanism of choice was escape. I had run away from parents who didn't love me, from people who told me I didn't measure up to their standards and needs, from any person or situation that made my life miserable. I had finally outgrown the asthma and allergies that had dogged my childhood. I'd left the home where I was considered weird and unlovable. I had escaped a disastrous first marriage that I'd made in a futile attempt to please my ever-critical mother.

In 1970, having broken up with a boyfriend I loved because my mother found him unsuitable, I married a man I couldn't stand because she told me it would make her immensely happy. Marrying Jack was an indication of my insanity, the worst thing that ever happened to me, aside from losing my sight. I left the marriage within months, without letting my mother know. Ironically, my pessimistic grandmother, who took such pleasure in others' sorrows, supported my decision to divorce Jack. A political and moral liberal, she did not equate love and sex; she saw no sanctity in a miserable marriage. Pragmatic to the core, she believed you got out of life only what luck and ambition could bring. To her way of thinking, an education and financial independence were far more important than a husband, and she saw me trying to achieve them. When my grandmother called the following year to tell me that my mother had committed suicide, I felt like I'd been set free, from her and from the marriage. "I can get a divorce" was the first thought that crossed my mind.

Now I had a successful, attractive husband who loved me. We had a lovely suburban home, late-model cars, and the usual amenities of a comfortable life. I was a highly regarded professional, with a lucrative career. We socialized with our friends. I was normal. I was like everyone else, although I still ran away when trouble loomed. Over the years, I'd tested Al's devotion through many trials, and he'd always passed with flying colors. How many times had I jumped in my car and run away? How many times had he come after me, proving that he was not like my family, demonstrating that he loved me and would care for me no matter what? I needed that escape hatch. I needed that reassurance. I needed my car. There was no way I was going back. But I could see that maintaining control of my life was going to take some doing.

The reactions of my doctors and coworkers showed me how awful it was to be disabled. As much as I resented their treatment, I had to admit that, until I joined the ranks of the handicapped, my own attitude toward blindness and disability had been no better. I could not imagine how anyone could survive, much less enjoy such a diminished life. I had begun to notice that there were few blind people out and about in the world. I rarely saw someone with a white cane or a guide dog in the street. I had never met a blind person, and I don't think I even knew anyone who knew someone blind. In fact, I had never met anyone with a disability. On the street, I gave ample clearance to people in wheelchairs. I pitied them.

When I began to have vision problems, I would casually ask people what they thought of the blind. Their responses often reflected their own fear and superstition. People would quote passages from the Bible about blindness as a retribution for sin, such as this line from Kings: "Smite this people, I pray, with blindness." They'd bring up the curse of blindness or the evil eye, and cite all manner of dismal historical references to blindness.

Some people shared their feelings of awkwardness around the disabled, admitting that they felt more comfortable keeping a distance. They were thankful it wasn't them, and did not like being reminded that "such things" could happen to them. Attempting to point out the positive aspects of blindness, they would mention Stevie Wonder or Ray Charles, who wrote marvelous music "despite the fact" that they were blind. Like me, they believed that it would be impossible to be happy, or even content, without vision.

A part of me acknowledged that there were enlightened people who accepted that someone disabled had worth, or talent, or a place in society. Unfortunately, I was not one of them. I was not up to the challenge of finding a place for myself in their world. I couldn't try to make my way again, with such a seemingly insurmountable handicap. The blind were cursed, and I was blind.

My own prejudices and the negative reinforcement of others' opinions compounded the dread that was creeping over me. The cold numbness protecting my sanity and equilibrium was thawing into a profound depression. I didn't talk about my feelings, and the people around me were afraid to ask about my emotional state. We all pretended that I was fine. I had erected an impenetrable fortress around myself, and I, and everyone in my force field, was a prisoner of my own defenses. Only in hindsight do I have any perspective on my extreme behavior.

Unlike clinical depression, situational depression is easy to hide. You can pawn your symptoms off as the trauma of the disaster itself—the accident, the illness, the divorce. Losing my sight was a perfectly legitimate reason for depression. Wouldn't anyone be depressed? I wasn't tearful, wasn't complaining or bemoaning my fate. Out loud or in public, that is. I was getting up (with Al's help) and getting dressed (with Al's help) and going to work and going to doctors. I was just extremely lethargic, pinned to the spot by a profound melancholy. Every movement, every breath, and every thought was like running a marathon while wearing hundred-pound ankle weights. The Herculean effort to deny the reality of my situation was taking its toll. I was escaping into an agitated and dreamless sleep for at least twelve hours a day. The doctors thought this was fine. Sleep meant that I was repairing after so many months of insomnia.

Actually, my prolonged bouts of drugged sleep were not conducive to recovery and success. I knew that my hyper-vigilance had been trumped, finally, by the depression. I still did not understand that my best option was to deal with my situation head-on, without the extremes of denial or hysterics. My options had narrowed, along with my central vision, but adaptation wasn't on my list.

By the end of November, the doctors were pretty certain that I'd had an episode of temporal arteritis. Also called giant cell arteritis, it is an inflammation of the arteries of the head, neck, and optic nerve that causes pain, headaches, and vision loss. They began to look for a more logical diagnosis, as they were still committed to the (since discredited) theory that temporal arteritis affects only males over the age of sixty-five.

When you lose your vision, you lose the world. Many people who go blind later in life commit suicide. Others implode, living their lives in the blind community, with whatever assistance—personal or institutional—they can find. Confined mostly to their room or home, they master only the skills they need to survive, reducing life to the barest essentials. This response is not surprising. When you first lose your sight, it's all you can do to breathe. Your body throbs with sensations that you can't escape for one second. There is only a boundless emptiness beyond the surface of your skin. You are a tiny island in an uncharted sea, able to connect only to what is within arm's reach. There is no world beyond your fingertips, unless you literally move to explore it. You no longer belong in the world "out there." There is only you "in here." You become profoundly aware that your personal reality is dependent on context. But all context has disappeared, and you are struck by how insignificant you are in the total scheme of things. You are the tree that has fallen in the forest with no one to hear it. I believed that in the absence of vision, I had morphed into a lump of protoplasm without purpose or soul. The air was being sucked out of my world, and what remained was a vacuum. The void always beckoned. The crushing pressure on my chest never let up. What choice did I really have but to function as if I had sight? As if my life still had meaning?

I continued to force myself to extremes. Every ounce of my energy was expended on the scam of making myself appear normal, viable, and still a participant in the game. Get dressed and get on the commuter van, sit straight at my desk, make my voice sound normal and strong. *Good morning. Thanks so much. Let's do that a little later. That sounds like fun.* Inhale, exhale. Repeat.

Asking for help was out of the question. No one had ever helped me. By the age of six, I'd understood that there was no one to trust except myself. If I made myself small, did not complain, did not ask for anything or express a desire, I would not be emotionally vulnerable. I could maintain the illusion that my life was under my control. I would not have to endure my parents' wrath or rejection. And of course I would not have to face the crushing knowledge of their indifference. I could manage.

Now, having learned no more effective survival strategies, I naturally fell back on my infantile defense mechanisms. Silence was my best ally. I couldn't trust anyone to see my weakness, because I couldn't risk rejection. I convinced myself, in the face of all evidence to the contrary, that if I dealt with the continual changes with zest and aplomb *everything* would be all right. It was hard to keep my composure, though, because I was never alone. At work I was always within earshot of my coworkers. Dozens of uncaring strangers rode the commuter van. At home, I was with Al every minute. Sad to say, I believed that only my beloved white standard poodle, Nova, really knew what I was feeling about the horrible changes occurring in my life. Nova was my only confidante.

The monumental effort of rudimentary functioning left me no energy or desire to learn the new skills required to adjust to my disability. I was too exhausted keeping up appearances to learn how to organize my clothes or make a sandwich. After all, why did I have to relearn the activities of daily living if my blindness was going to turn out to be nothing more than a bad dream? I had Al to sustain my illusions. At home Al did everything for me. *Al, get me a blanket. Al, bring me a glass of water. Read this article to me. Find my green blouse.*

Looking back, I don't believe I even said "please" or "thank you"! Acknowledging Al's help would have forced me to acknowledge my helplessness. Besides, did he have a problem? Al loved me. He knew I was blind! Everyone knows that the blind are totally dependent on others to have their needs met. Of course what Al really wanted was to *help* me do this and *teach* me to do that. But I hadn't the energy to do anything more than breathe and sleep, and simulate doing my job. Learning new skills was beyond the scope of my energy and psyche.

Lurking behind my depression was the repressed cauldron of emotion I kept so well hidden. I was angry. No, furious! Why had this happened to me? Hadn't I done everything possible to ensure a calm and comfortable life? I needed to grieve, to reflect on all I'd lost, to understand what life without sight would be like, what the label of blindness meant to me. I desperately needed to cry my way through boxes and boxes of Kleenex. A less damaged person would have talked about her fears, cried and ranted and asked for help, and given herself time to come to terms with her fate. For all Al's caring—caring that I took for granted—he did not understand the depths of my denial. During the six months prior to being labeled "blind" I had fervently and privately nourished the hope that I would awaken from this nightmare and everything would be back to normal. How could I mourn a loss that I refused to acknowledge? How could I prepare for a loss that surely was transitory? I nurtured the faith that if I held on long enough I would emerge from this abyss.

I was between the proverbial rock and a hard place. My old tricks were useless. I couldn't just get up and leave, because I couldn't drive. Al had taken away my car keys. I pretended I was independent, even though I couldn't find the toothpaste without Al's help. I counted on Al not only to keep me alive and wearing my clothes right side out, but to uphold my version of reality. Al kept telling me that I needed to get some rehabilitation training so that I could negotiate my new world. I kept trying to prove to him that his advice was ludicrous, insisting that I could still function on my own. At the time my behavior seemed rational, not desperate and foolish. When I think back to those days I know why my husband had had enough.

I have dozens of examples of my impossible behavior that would be hysterically funny if they weren't so pathetic and, at times, dangerous. For example, trying to cook dinner one night, I inadvertently jammed something between the freezer door and the seal. By the time Al came inside from cutting the lawn, the entire freezer had defrosted and the ice machine had melted all over the kitchen floor. The freezer was a pool of water intermixed with wrappers from the freezer boxes and blood from the defrosting meat.

Then there was the time I had a fierce craving for microwave popcorn. No problem, except that I put the popcorn bag in the microwave wrong side up. Then I hit the wrong timer button. I went to the bathroom and emerged to the smell of something burning. By the time I groped my way back to the kitchen, the popcorn and its bag were a charred heap of ashes. Everything in the house reeked of Jiffy-Pop, and the microwave was ruined.

Only days later, in an attempt to fix scrambled eggs and hash browns for myself, I apparently poured too much oil into the hot pan and turned the flame up too high. Realizing I had set the kitchen on fire, I panicked and began screaming. I marveled to myself at the usefulness of vision. *If I could see, I wouldn't have started this fire in the first place, and if I could see I probably could have put it out. But nooo, I'm blind.* Fortunately, a neighbor working in his yard came running, grabbed the fire extinguisher, and put out the grease fire. When Al returned from Wal-Mart to witness the devastation of yet another one of my independence fiascos, he was livid. He forbade me to use the stove until I had taken some rehabilitation classes. Not the dreaded word *rehabilitation. No way.*

Naturally, the next time I was left alone in the house I headed straight for the stove. This time there was a dish towel at the edge of the burner that Al had used to clean up grease and powder from the extinguisher. The towel and the back wall of the kitchen and a bank of cabinets went up in flames. This stubborn act cost us eight thousand dollars. Al and I did not speak to each other for a week. I was furious with him for carelessly leaving a towel on the stove. I think this is called grasping at straws. He seemed to feel that the fire and the possible damage I could have caused to myself, let alone to our home, was a more legitimate reason to assign blame. He still cannot talk about that day without getting angry.

Okay, so the stove was off-limits. How about the oven? The oven shouldn't be such a problem, right? One night, Al decided to broil lamb chops and set them up on the counter while he was cutting vegetables for a salad. He asked me please not to help, but to simply stand there and talk with him. Why did he think I couldn't be of help? When he left the kitchen, I decided to put the lamb chops in the broiler and turn on the oven. I found the oven, but I couldn't figure out how to line up the metal rack or how to adjust the dials. The world was fading fast, and I'd done nothing to prepare for the loss.

By this time I had an assigned social worker from the Texas Commission for the Blind, my diagnosis having been made a matter of legal record. Susan Poff had a thankless job. I refused to attend classes in orientation and mobility or Braille. I refused to enroll at the Criss Cole Rehabilitation Center in Austin, where they teach life skills in a residency program that helps the newly blind adult transition. I was, however, dragged into the office of a counselor who specialized in dealing with sudden blindness. Her suggestion was that since I was having so much difficulty at work, I quit my job and focus solely on me.

Uh-uh. That was not my plan. How could I relinquish my job or enter rehabilitation when I still wasn't ready to be a blind person? My medical care was eating up our life savings. Both my self-esteem and my economic responsibilities demanded that I keep working. Rather than be pitied or rejected, I would, all by myself, become the perfect blind person before going public. I got tapes from the Hadley School for the Blind and secretly set about learning Braille and everyday skills. I would learn to cook and sew, do the laundry, and organize my clothes. How hard could it be to relearn a few basic skills on my own? The answer to this question is: nearly impossible. Reality struck when Al stopped putting out my clothes.

Finally I had to face the inevitable. Prior to losing my sight I could multitask with the best of them. I could simultaneously talk on the phone, use a computer, add a column of figures in my head, drink a cup of coffee, and chew gum. Now I was two years old again, learning to walk and talk and feed myself. Each small ordinary task of daily living presented a massive learning challenge. Every additional yard I learned to navigate felt like a mile. There were thousands of these once no-brainer tasks to be remastered: putting on underwear right side out, squeezing toothpaste onto a brush, rinsing my mouth, replacing the cup in its holder, eating peas, putting a teaspoon of sugar in my tea, drinking from a glass, using a remote control, buttoning a shirt, zipping a jacket, unscrewing a bottle top, and using a can opener. Simple motions I'd taken for granted, basic acts of coordination, became hurdles to overcome. It took me two weeks to learn to put toothpaste on a brush without getting most of it on my hands and the sink. I had to learn to distinguish tubes by their size, squeeze patterns, weight, and caps. I had to remember to hold the cap in my hand, so I could put it back on the toothpaste before losing it. I had to train myself, and Al, to put everything back in the same place, in the same order, every single time, without fail. For a person who is essentially a slob, this obsessive behavior was quite a challenge.

Every object in our environment required that I learn to identify it and to use it: socks, nylons, underwear, T-shirts, dresses,
combs, brushes, handbags, forks, spoons, cups, plates, cans,
bottles, doors, drawers, lamps, vases, pens, and paper. There
was no end to the world's stuff, and thus no end to my reeducation.

All this was very slow going indeed. When the world no
longer comes to you through your eyes, you have to go out
and move through the world in order to understand it. You
have to connect Point A with Point B, whether those points
represent the distance between two objects on your bedside
table or the distance between you and your office.
Unfortunately, my lack of mobility and orientation training was
a major hindrance. I was still closely tethered to my bed and
desk. Days, weeks, and months ticked by as my sight continued
to fade, and I wasn't getting any more mobile. How much easier my life would have been if I could have simply said, *I am
blind and I need help.*

By now I could no longer distinguish between two pairs of
shoes with a similar shape, or find the bathroom in the house
I'd lived in for eight years without groping the walls and tripping over the furniture. I could no longer see my face in the
mirror. By the time I dressed every morning and boarded the
commuter van, I had already expended my daily energy quota
on the immensely complex tasks of brushing my teeth and hair,
dressing, and making an attempt at breakfast. My daily ration
of emotional resources was already depleted.

Al and I were barely speaking. Having studied psychology
in college, he decided that his help was a hindrance to my
progress. He stopped feeding me and fetching for me. It may

well have been the right tactic, but he was also plenty irritated. His life was no picnic either, and our carefully ordered life together was in shambles. His companion and playmate had all but disappeared, replaced by a disabled, angry wife. The extraordinary level of day-to-day caretaking was getting to him, especially given my lack of appreciation and my refusal to seek rehabilitation. Our usual, almost imperceptible bickering level escalated to harsh criticism and complaint. There were no pleasant moments in our warped world, and we were headed for divorce.

In January 1994, Al was transferred to duty at Camp Pendleton, California. We were both relieved. Free of Al's nagging, I was just fine, thank you. Now I could spend all day hating the world, and all night in sweet oblivion. Or, in clinical terms, mired in profound depression. Susan, my social worker, took the opportunity of Al's absence to try to convince me to enroll in some basic classes. She thought that my reluctance to admit I was blind was in part based on my fear of losing Al's approval. She knew that Al had wanted me near him and had been reluctant to have me go off to the Criss Cole Center for months of rehabilitation. She hoped that by the time he returned, in late June, I would have learned orientation and mobility, and some basic life skills. Al's anger, his refusal to go for counseling, and his abandonment of me had shocked her. She felt that his insensitivity to my loss was aggravating my depression.

I knew better. Given my behavior, his abdication made perfect sense. Urging me to gain my independence now that my monster husband was gone, Susan dragged me to mobility classes, insisting I learn to use a cane. "You have to make a decision," she said. "Do you want to be a blind person in a blind world or a blind person in the sighted world?"

She kept repeating this admonition, but I didn't get it. By now I was barely eating and had dropped below ninety pounds. I had severe asthma and other medical problems, but I refused medical care. At work, I spoke only when absolutely necessary. When I was not at work trying to avoid some contact that would betray my incompetence, I was home trying to find my way to the bedroom so I could go to sleep and escape my life. The only task I did every day was let my dear Nova out, feed her, and cuddle with her before crawling into bed. No lights in the house, the only sound the panting of the dog. My desire for sleep was so strong that I resented the sounds of the birds, the noises of lawn mowers, of children playing, the reminders of sighted life. I had not chosen this prison of blindness and was furious about having to live within its bars.

Going to work every day remained the core component of my denial, the last tattered threads of my emotional security blanket. But now I had to deal with the opposition. My boss announced that he was assigning me a new work space, and I was escorted from my corner office overlooking the atrium park to a windowless storage room piled to the ceiling with boxes. What did it matter to me, they explained, since I couldn't see it anyway. No one expected me to do any work anymore, and the hospital refused to retrain me, or to provide an adaptive computer.

None of my coworkers said a word. No one came into my office or offered to assist me to the cafeteria or bathroom. I was left to my own devices. Not surprising, since I'd had no intimate pals to begin with and I had rebuffed anyone who tried to offer help. No matter. I needed to hold that job under any conditions, having still found no alternative that I could tolerate. It was a standoff.

No work crossed my desk. I was not informed of staff meetings, and when I met someone in the halls or bathroom, I could not engage them in conversation. Occasionally, my immediate boss would poke his head in to see if I had made it into work. Usually, however, days would go by and I would not talk to anyone. My isolation increased and, with it, my dread. I dragged myself to work each morning, heavy-limbed and lethargic. I listened to audiobooks, slept sitting up, or practiced my Braille until ten hours had passed and I could return home to my seclusion and solitude.

I have to admit there was a bit of a dance going on, in which my employers and I colluded. I was trying to act as if I wasn't blind and could do my job. They were only too happy to use my behavior as evidence that I was faking blindness in order to get disability compensation.

The Texas Commission for the Blind sent a technology specialist to my workplace, explaining that the state would provide adaptive equipment and training. The employer's sole responsibility was cooperation and patience, but my bosses wanted no part of this process. The hospital already employed the required number of disabled persons, so it had no further obligation to comply with the law. Management was upset that the hospital was stuck with someone blind, yet paying for a full-time employee. They did not want a guide dog in their facility and refused to expedite the changes that would have made it an adaptive workplace. No matter what my social worker said to them, no matter how many times she tried to educate or intervene, despite the fact that my medical documents proved I was blind, my employers were convinced that I was faking my sudden disability. They couldn't understand why I would want to work or why I would want people to see me in this state. It was a Catch-22 predicament. They wanted a functioning employee, and I wanted to function; neither was possible.

The dreaded day came when my boss informed me that his department no longer had any use for my services. Though my prior evaluation had been exemplary, he said, the hospital had done a reevaluation, and had decided that I was no longer able to function in my job capacity. My employers expressed concern that they could find no obvious reason for my poor performance. They wanted me to reflect on the reasons for my decline, and had decided it would be best if I accepted a reassignment. Wary of Americans with Disabilities Act ramifications, they were not going to fire me. Two can play this game, they were saying. You pretend you're blind, and we'll pretend you're faking it. I was caught in my own deception. I was faking competence, and they were only too happy to play along with my lame act to prove their own case.

I was to be transferred to any department that would take me. Based on the fact that I looked normal and could still utilize proper body language, they expected me to be capable of reading and filing reports or working with computers. But if I couldn't find my way to the bathroom or cafeteria, if I had to count the steps between doors to find the correct office, how was I to read patient charts or do calculations, without adaptive equipment?

One day I happened to meet the woman who administered the hospital's pension plan in the ladies' room. An independent agent who was about to make a transitional move to Dallas, she became my ally. For the next several months, Martha would come by my office at lunchtime and take me to the cafeteria.

She carried my tray, and I followed with my cane, placing one arm on her shoulder as a guide. When we passed the table where my former coworkers ate, she would pointedly say hello, showing her disdain when they ignored my existence. Occasionally, in the middle of the workday afternoon she would take me shopping or to a movie.

It was nice to have someone on my side, but it was clearly an untenable situation. I was just going through the motions. Numb, depressed, exhausted, emotionally drained, I was wishing for a miracle whose form I could not have articulated. I hated the way I was being treated, hated the attitude of the hospital toward the disabled and toward me in particular. I resented their outright refusal to permit the Texas Commission for the Blind to introduce adaptive equipment into the workplace, and their contention that purchasing two ten-dollar signs to mark the bathrooms as handicapped accessible could not be easily expedited. I was tired of my boss reminding me, when we spoke at all, that I should "appreciate his position," that his departmental performance rating was declining because I was blind. Why didn't I just take a disability retirement and make his life easier? I was affecting his bottom line and he was angry. Why couldn't I live on the disability payment of $667 a month, pre-tax? What needs could I possibly have now that I was blind? He kept stating that I was making his life miserable because I wanted to work. Because I wanted a place in society. Because I wanted desperately to maintain the status quo, which I was unwilling to admit had already eluded me. My social worker kept insisting that I had rights and needed to exercise them. Finally I understood that the "I can still see" game was over and, with the support of my social worker, approached Access Austin to help me. I would sue the hospital for the right to be rehabilitated. The only good news in all this was it would force me to accept the label of *blind*.

Then fate intervened. At three A.M. one night in May, the phone rang. It was the chief of cardiovascular surgery at Balboa Naval Hospital in San Diego, informing me that Al had become short of breath while jogging. He had been shipped via ambulance from Camp Pendleton and was now in the coronary intensive care unit. The doctors suspected that his arteries were 80 to 90 percent blocked. They needed to perform a cardiac catheterization, and he would probably require open-heart surgery. I'd better come to the hospital as soon as possible.

In that moment the whole rickety edifice of my charade came crashing down. It was suddenly clear to me that I deeply loved Al, and I needed to be at his side. It was also clear to me that I was incapable of making a plane reservation, and had not a friend I could call to help me get to the airport. Here was the line in the sand of my denial. It was not bravery that caused me to pick up the phone but, rather, the knowledge that Al and I were part of a team whose members relied on each other for love and support. My heart in my throat, I dialed the operator. "Can you help me?" I said. *"I'm blind."*

CHAPTER THREE

SHADOW PLAY

Art teaches nothing, except the significance of life.

—HENRY MILLER

My TERROR ONLY PARTLY MASKED by my fear that Al would die, I got myself to the hospital in San Diego. My ophthalmologist's nurse, whom I'd woken at five A.M. (and whose kindness I will never forget), packed my things, shoved my cane in my hand, drove me to the airport, and turned me over to other kind people who got me on the plane. That plane ride was a pivotal lesson in the unrelenting moment-to-moment complexity of a blind person's life. A blind person who might choose, as my social worker kept pointing out, to live in the world of the sighted. This was my coming-out party.

I was remanded to the care of strangers who changed their levels of responsibility so swiftly that I did not even have time to catch their names. The flight attendant quizzed me to ascertain my level of comprehension and sight. Relieved to discover that I was oriented and in full control of my faculties, she nevertheless insisted that for safety reasons I move to a bulkhead seat in the first-class cabin. So I was moved. Handled. I recoiled when, without warning, someone suddenly reached down to assist me with the seat belt. Announcements I was too frazzled to understand were made, and the plane took off. I hadn't mastered the art of eating or drinking at home, so I certainly couldn't manage it on an airplane, around strangers whose clothing and computers I might endanger, whose territory I might violate. I couldn't get up to go to the bathroom. Unmoored from my familiar surroundings, I struggled to make sense of this vast uncharted land that was to be my new world. Could others sense my panic?

Another kind stranger helped me off the plane and into the terminal. With only a cane, handbag, and carry-on bag, disembarking was not difficult. No need for baggage claim or a trip in the motorized cart to another terminal. But now what?

It was Airport 101. I had often flown before but had forgotten, or had just accepted in my previous life, the chaos of an airport terminal. Los Angeles International Airport is a city unto itself, capable of rendering even the sighted confused, anxious, and impatient. Announcements of departure gates, late arrivals, and terminal changes are indecipherable, and the bustling crowds avoid collision only through the agency of sight.

How quickly you lose the world without continuous and automatic visual reinforcement. You don't need to memorize what you can always see at will. How quickly I had forgotten about escalators and moving walkways, about transport carts and telephone kiosks. About life. It is doubly hard to keep your wits about you when you can't see. I was in a perpetual state of perplexity.

Twenty-four hours earlier I could barely make it from my bed to my bathroom, and it was still taking me over an hour to dress. Now speed and orientation were at a premium, and I had neither. My belongings and I made for a little dark outpost in this chaos. Was I near a stairway? The entrance? Was I blocking traffic flow? My bladder reminded me that I had not been in a bathroom since early morning. I'd had nothing to eat, and didn't know if I had enough money or time to purchase something. How would I do that, in any case? Was I permitted to ask an airline employee to help me? What were the denominations of the bills in my wallet, and how would I know the choices, prices, the appropriate change? *How dependent can I be without being a victim?* Was I supposed to know something about this airport, airline, and flight before I got on the plane? Where was I supposed to go? Why hadn't I prepared? *Why is this happening to me?* The questions tumbled over one another. I wanted to scream. This simple trip required a level of competence that I hadn't encountered before, a level of blind functionality that I'd assiduously avoided. It was all too much.

Al's brother Jim found me frozen in my pool of darkness, clinging to my bag and my last shred of sanity. He was shocked to learn that I couldn't see. Yet another victim of my secrecy. Nor had I prepared him for the time away from his work, for the need to rent a car and drive me from Los Angeles to the hospital in San Diego—the need to do everything for me. To play Al's role.

We arrived at the hospital as they wheeled Al in for the cardiac catheterization, just in time for a kiss and a few words. He had signed the permit for the procedure but had refused to give written permission for open-heart surgery, convinced (not without historical precedent) that I was being overly dramatic and that the doctors were exaggerating the probability of major surgery. Al had been in the procedure room less than an hour when the surgeon came out and informed us of Al's urgent need for open-heart surgery. They needed me to sign permission papers.

"What papers?"

"These papers here; we need you to sign them."

"Where?"

"Here. On the dotted line."

"You'll have to show me," I said, admitting for the second time that day, *"I can't see."*

Al's surgery to unblock his arteries went well—except that he had a heart attack and a stroke on the operating table. After days in intensive care he was transferred to a cardiac step-down unit. It was not until then that the doctors, nurses, and military personnel began to notice that Al had come out of surgery with stroke deficits that required close monitoring. A week later, he had another stroke, and the problems mounted. He experienced long stretches of memory loss and the inability to find and formulate words. He would pick up the telephone to call someone and not realize until an hour later that he was still in the process of trying to execute the call. He would forget who someone was, or be unable to identify the use for a common object. He was physically weak and needed assistance with all major tasks. He was emotionally labile, veering from giddiness to rage in the course of a minute. While he could often name an object correctly or complete a sentence, at times his language consisted entirely of four-letter words, causing him much distress. He knew that his behavior was inappropriate but could do little to control it. It would be many weeks before Al was healthy enough for discharge and further at-home rehabilitation. Fortunately, he was under excellent care.

The real problem was Al's helpless blind wife. In California I realized that it was in fact possible to live without sight, and I discovered that people of goodwill were there to help me learn how to do so. Jim was an angel in disguise. I know now that without his aid, without his acceptance of my situation and my peculiar way of handling Al's illness, I would never have survived the initial weeks. He did not pry into my level of blindness but just accepted me as me, complete with my denial and skill deficits. Jim's emotional support gave me the calm space I needed to deal with my situation moment by moment. While Al recuperated from his surgery and strokes, I was taking a primer course in living in the sighted world.

My disability qualified me for housing on hospital grounds, where services were provided for family members who needed assistance. The military ran a type of Ronald McDonald house for families of hospitalized active-duty personnel, and this is where I stayed throughout the ten weeks of Al's hospitalization. Meals were prepared and the beds were made, to name just two of the many things I still hadn't learned to do.

As to the rest, necessity forced me to invent my own rehabilitation program. You'd be surprised how difficult the simple act of walking becomes when you are blind. It is so easy to slip in that split second between putting one foot down and picking up the other, even with close attention. Introduce a loose rock, a bit of sand, or just a little water, mixed with a moment's inattention, and, *kaboom,* you are flat on your bum. I can't tell you how many times I've sure-stepped myself into a sitting position at the bottom of a stairway. Until you get over your fear of falling, your muscles are tight, your nerves are on edge. You feel like you're walking a tightrope on the edge of a precipice.

I found my own cockamamie strategy for walking down stairs, carefully placing my heel against the back of every riser. This is not what they teach you in orientation and mobility class. You're supposed to use your cane to feel out the stair in front of you. I discovered that counting steps to the bathroom, down a hall, or through a courtyard could get me more or less where I wanted to go. I taught myself to get across the open courtyards connecting the hospital buildings by moving straight ahead as the crow flies. These techniques are not correct form, but they would put me in range of my destination. Then all I had to do was stand there and wait until someone came up and asked me if I needed assistance. Not that I would ask for help, mind you; I hadn't yet reached that advanced stage. But just acknowledging to myself that I needed assistance was a shocking leap forward.

The social worker assigned to Al also took me under his wing. He had someone do the grocery shopping for me and go with me to stores for underwear, sundries, and medications. He had someone teach me to use the base services, to find the cafeterias and gym. When Al was ready for his first excursions outside the hospital wards, the social worker made certain a sighted person went along, until he was assured that I could find my way around. He had someone translate for me the informational chirping sounds at intersection lights and explain the proper strategy for crossing streets, cautioning me not to attempt it on my own unless someone sighted was with me, or until I had formal training.

I did not seriously heed his warning until the day Al had a temper tantrum at the San Diego Zoo. He had been given a day pass, and the doctor had suggested that we go to a public environment that he would enjoy. We took a bus to the zoo. Bought some peanuts to feed the elephants. Walked around while Al described the sights and I absorbed the sounds and smells. All in all a lovely day, until Al decided he wanted to get the car and drive home. There was no car, of course, and we were not home in Georgetown, Texas. But this rare outing had tired him, and nothing I said or did could convince him of these facts. As his fatigue increased, so did his confusion and his irrational behavior. Desperate to calm him, I suggested that we walk to the car (the base was only a few blocks away). Having visited the zoo several times before with Jim, I was sure I could find my way back, with Al reading the street signs to me.

I was wrong. Al was unable to read the signs in his agitated state, and I could not accurately interpret the chirping messages of the intersection buttons. Al was now screaming that he couldn't find the car keys, cursing and yelling insults at the top of his lungs. Angry and desperate to avoid a scene, I unwittingly pulled us into a bustling intersection, where a police car nearly ran us over. The policeman jumped out, yelling at us, and I broke into tears. By the time I'd stopped crying, he had delivered us to the main gate and into the hands of the military police, who in turn delivered us to the entrance of the hospital, with a lecture about sensible behavior. I left Al in the hands of a kindly nurse, who medicated my bellowing husband and tucked him safely into bed. I sat on a chair in Al's hospital room, too numb to move.

My reeducation proceeded. Helpful strangers showed me how to use a credit card at the PX, where I bought sweats so I could use the treadmill at the gym. At the commissary I relearned the complex mechanics of eating with a knife and fork. I devised a system for marking my clothes and organizing them in drawers. Just as they were about to discharge Al, he had another stroke. By the time we returned to Georgetown, Al had short-term memory loss, significant speech deficits, and dramatic mood swings that were sometimes frightening.

Back at home, I struggled to cope without the support of Al's brother and the hospital personnel. I was forced to reach out to strangers every time we needed to make a trip to the pharmacy or grocery store. I say "we" because Al and I were a tandem team, with Al providing the vision, and me the memory.

Any outing, even a simple trip to the supermarket, could suddenly go badly awry. With me tagging along to make sure we
got everything on our list, Al would throw an ear-splitting
tantrum when he couldn't find the cereal that was on the shelf
directly in front of him. He'd pick fights with strangers because
he couldn't understand why he had to wait in line. Variations in
prices confused him, and he'd be overwhelmed by the need to
select one product over another. He was incapable of following
directions and confused by crowds. Stamping his feet like a
two-year-old and throwing a temper tantrum at the slightest
provocation was his norm in those days. The only silver lining
to this cloud was that now he was the identified patient, and I
was, by default, able to assume the role of caretaker.

We were officially in rehabilitation now—for Al. We stepped
into a steady stream of clinical psychologists and other rehabili-
tative services. Al went through endless hours of psychological
tests to determine the extent of his losses. Then it was hours a
day of speech therapy, cognitive therapy, occupational therapy,
cardiac rehab, and psychotherapy. I accompanied him on every
visit. Then Al had a fourth stroke, and for a short time he completely lost the ability to speak. *If there is such a thing as a living
hell, this surely must be it,* I thought. Part of me was numb. I
was not depressed—the unrelenting activity was staving off
depression. But I was overwhelmed. I wanted to escape the
responsibility for every decision made during every waking
moment of every day. Spending every minute with Al, in sole
charge of his schedule and his medications, took all my energy.
I was tired of being responsible for interpreting his speech and
overseeing his behavior. I rued the day I'd complained that
most of his speech was profanity; now he was mostly silent. I
dreamed of fleeing to a tropical island piled to the tops of the
palm trees with the books I so sorely missed.

Everyone offered a remedy for Al's condition. The neuropsychologist suggested that we enroll in foreign-language classes. The cognitive therapist suggested mapmaking. The speech therapist suggested Post-it notes on every object. Desperate for a way out of this hell, I enrolled him in every rehabilitation protocol suggested, and attended every session. It was grueling, but taking care of Al made me feel needed again. Not to mention that dealing with Al's needs kept me from facing the fact that my remaining central vision and color perception were falling below measurable levels.

I could write a book about living with someone who's had a stroke. It was typical for me to have to repeat a question or command to Al fifteen times before I would get a verbal response, or before he could initiate a task. If he was interrupted while tackling a task, the process would begin again, and I'd have to repeat the original direction fifteen more times. Even today, when he is tired or stressed, the magic number is eight times. Being a caretaker is often a thankless and frustrating experience. You feel like a shrew, and find yourself preplanning and micromanaging every task as a way to preserve your sanity, and to accomplish what needs to be done. Patience is not a virtue in these circumstances, merely a defensive position. A sense of humor is invaluable in offsetting feelings of powerlessness over the situation.

Al's memory loss had a way of distorting reality. Inaccurate dates, times, persons, and places were the norm, so constant reinforcement of the correct information was critical. Al's problem with time distortion went beyond simple acts like placing the car keys on the kitchen counter and spending minutes trying to remember where they were. The disassociation undermined my confidence in his ability to make a concrete decision and exercise common sense. Every one of Al's deficits was compounded by my own blindness.

Al had periods of lucidity mixed with periods of dense emotional fog. My problem was learning to anticipate, discriminate, and adjust. I quickly learned not to take his behavior personally. He might fail to complete a task and not remember until two or three hours or days later that he hadn't finished what he'd started. This awareness after the fact made him lovable but unreliable, though he sometimes reacted to his failures with outbursts of temper and paranoia. At times the answer to a question would be locked in his brain, and the response would not emerge for minutes or hours. Then he would blurt out the answer to a mystified audience that had moved on to a completely different topic. Other times he would interrupt a conversation to parrot someone else's answer, going on at length, truly believing that everyone was politely listening to him, when they were actually waiting for a verbal pause so they could walk away. When Al awakened to his social ineptitude, he'd be embarrassed.

Dealing with someone who has a disability that is not physically obvious can be more difficult than dealing with a noticeable deficit. A stroke victim may present no apparent physical clues to his condition. When Al has an emotional flare-up, everyone wonders where it came from. Did they miss some obvious social cue? I sometimes wonder if Al is mentally present or away somewhere watering the lawn. Should I provide a verbal cue of inappropriate behavior, or is this cruel? Am I being overprotective or truly helping him avoid harm? It's a problem that never has a resolution. It's often when you lose your patience or sense of humor and abdicate your protective role that your loved one comes to harm.

When people do the unexpected, it makes you question your own reality. Every time Al squirrels away a piece of paper or opens the mail, I cringe. Every time he uses his ATM card and fails to remember the amount or the incident, I feel a tiny decline in my emotional security. I reassess how much control is necessary to preserve my own well-being and still foster his independence. This is true especially because my own well-being requires constant vigilance just for me to get through the day.

Al's ability to speak and formulate words and sentences began to improve with the help of the foreign-language classes, which seemed to open new channels in his brain. He began to relate words to objects and could eventually complete a concrete sentence and articulate a need. Once he'd reestablished coherent speech, we traveled to San Antonio for weekly sessions with the cognitive therapist. The therapist determined that Al had permanently lost his ability to do anything beyond simple math, to accurately relate dates and historical events, and to remember issues and ideas on a short-term basis. Al's emotional outbursts, his long sulking spells, and his expectation that others adjust to his emotions began to improve. The doctors believed he would regain his ability to consider others in basic matters of politeness, patience, and common courtesy. "Give it time," the therapist kept repeating. I kept thinking, *How long?* Soon the doctors decided that Al was ready for physical rehabilitation, so three times a week Al had cardiac rehabilitation at the hospital were I was employed.

Yes, where I was employed. Believe it or not, I'd gone back to my job when we returned home, having taken the maximum allowable family emergency leave. My employers had assumed, or had fervently hoped, that between Al's dire situation and mine, crowned by their harassment and refusal to accommodate me, I would quietly disappear. *Actually, no.* I was still a blind person who had found no alternative life that was tolerable. The hospital management was not happy to see me, but what else was I going to do? At least now I could get myself to the bathroom and use a credit card. My socks probably matched. But between my exhaustion from meeting Al's needs and the hospital's continuing pressure, I lasted only another five weeks—just long enough for them to process the paperwork for disability retirement and send me happily out of their lives.

At this point, the military and the doctors determined that Al could begin to drive again under supervision—mine. As long as I knew our location at all times, he was given permission to get behind a wheel. By Christmas, the cognitive therapist declared that Al could draw and articulate an accurate map; his logic and sense of direction had returned. Now Al could drive to the grocery store, cleaners, and gas station without me.

I tried to be properly pleased about Al's recovery. The doctors kept reminding me that I could never expect him to learn to put anything away. Yes, I was blind, but I was reeducable, while he was incapable of adjusting. It was up to me to learn to work around him. This squeaky-wheel-gets-the-oil policy seemed an intolerable request. Why should I have to be the one to adjust? Don't I have enough to contend with? What about my own needs for support? *I'm blind, shouldn't I get help?*

My frustration grew and grew. I'd try to temper Al's behavior, reminding him when he was verbally inappropriate, when his sloppiness (which was now worse than mine) made maneuvering in the house impossible for me. One day, he cut someone off in a gas station and was soon embroiled in a shouting match. Instead of intervening, I prayed that the other driver would punch him and someone would call the police. Perhaps that would bring the months of intensive caretaking, of being the mediator and the overseer of common sense, to an end. Maybe someone would take pity on my plight. But no, the shouting subsided and we went home. I sunk into a depression so severe that no one thought I would come out of it.

It shows the depth of my despair that at this low point, in a desperate plea for solace, I called my father to tell him that I was blind. "So what do you want me to do about it?" he grumbled. *What had I been thinking?* This is a man who didn't interrupt his card game to call an ambulance when my mother died. A man who showed up late at the funeral of the son who worked for him for eighteen years, cried for two minutes, and left. This is a man who never bothered to learn his grandson's name or the name of his son's wife. My father and I could talk about the stock market or the economy. "The Dow went up sixty points today, isn't that great" passed for intimate conversation. We'd discuss his business, his travels, his life; he never asked about mine. A few times during my life, out of the blue, he told me that he loved me or was proud of me; each time I was shocked. Years earlier, I'd discovered that he secretly kept tabs on me; by some indirect means he'd find out that I'd graduated from college, was working as a trauma-care nurse, had moved, or had taken a new job. I guess I was holding out hope that he cared for me, despite his distance, and would respond to my need. Stunned by his indifference, I set the phone back in its cradle. That was the last time we ever spoke.

It was clear that there was no help for me. No one would come to my rescue now. I crawled into bed and refused to eat, rising only to go to the bathroom. For two months, I wore the same clothes and did not take a shower. After a month of this, Al stopped feeding my beloved Nova, forcing me to make daily trips to the kitchen. Feeding Nova was as much as I could muster. I was emotionally and physically ill.

———————————

When I finally went back to the doctors, theoretically because my cataracts had "ripened" to the point where they could perform an operation to remove them, my corneas had deteriorated so badly that transplants offered the only option for salvaging any remnant of my sight. *Salvage my sight?* I jumped at the chance. Whatever it required, I was going to see again. I would read. I would drive. I would buy a new car. I would escape the ghastly world of the blind and life with Al as a stroke victim. Over the next two months, energized by hope and dreams, I endured multiple surgeries without complaint.

Not to dwell on a shatteringly sad interlude, I did see again, for a brief bright few weeks in February 1995. I was able to watch TV and read large-print books. Books, my lifelong comfort food; I read and read. Here again, my mind ran on parallel tracks. Knowing that I might be seeing on borrowed time, a part of me paid close attention, savoring the world of ten thousand things. With my new eyes, I greedily devoured every one of the world's objects, every color, angle of light, and nuance of movement. I memorized every flower and sunset, every plane of Al's face. I took careful note of my surroundings, refreshing my memory of how everything worked, in case I would again descend into darkness. I restored my memories of people and places that had already begun to fade, taking mental notes. The most ordinary sight now seemed magical to me, miraculous.

The other half of my brain reveled in my restored vision, my restored life, convinced that the continuing vacillations in my vision were the normal side effects of surgery. I shopped for a new car. A Jaguar? A VW convertible?

When I went back to the doctor three weeks later to be fitted for new glasses, he spent a suspiciously long time trying to ascertain my vision levels. Things kept shifting, fading. Then they shifted again, and again. I couldn't see the color red. After an hour of this, my doctor slumped in his chair. "I think what you have is some form of vasculitis."

Finally, I had an explanation for my blindness, pretty much a worst-case scenario: a degenerative, systemic autoimmune disease that pursues me to this day.

Vasculitis is an autoimmune disease that produces inflammation of the blood vessels (the vascular system)—veins, arteries, and capillaries. It's a rare orphan disease, difficult to diagnose because the symptoms can mimic other diseases. Symptoms show up wherever blood vessels malfunction, which can be anywhere—from the eyes and ears to the heart and liver, to the central or peripheral nervous systems.

The treatment options depend on the severity of the disease. Mild cases of vasculitis are generally not life threatening. In some cases no treatment is required. Severe cases (involving major organs) are permanently disabling and fatal. Chemotherapy and prednisone, plasmapheresis and cyclosporine—all of which I now take—are needed to control its effects.

I was eventually found to have two types of vasculitis. One is called giant cell arteritis and affects the temporal arteries, which course along the side of the head in front of the ears; this kind causes pain and headaches. The other is Churg-Strauss syndrome; it involves the lungs, peripheral nerves, skin, kidneys, and heart.

Many aspects of vasculitis remain a mystery. Researchers know that the immune system attacks the arteries, causing infarctions or aneurysms that damage them. But they don't know why, when, or where an attack will occur. Because the nonspecific symptoms of giant cell arteritis can show up either gradually or suddenly, it is very difficult to diagnose. The vision losses caused by giant cell arteritis are irreversible if not immediately detected and treated. In my case, by the time the doctors figured out what was wrong with my eyes, it was too late for treatment to work.

For years the medical community was skeptical that autoimmune diseases even existed, since the idea of the body attacking itself defies common sense. Today it is understood that autoimmune diseases are caused by misfiring cells of the immune system. Genetic predisposition, overlapping diseases, and environmental factors are potential triggers for vasculitis. It now seems pretty clear that undiagnosed vasculitis was involved in both my mother's and my brother's deaths, though at the time they were attributed to other factors. My younger brother, Larry, plagued by health issues all his life, has been definitively diagnosed with vasculitis.

I had only a few more weeks of fluctuating vision. One morning in early April 1995, I woke with a blinding headache that no pain medication could touch. In agony, I felt my way to the kitchen for an ice pack. Propping myself up at the kitchen window, I looked up and saw a bright red cardinal, an apparition clear as day. Just at that moment, a lightning bolt of pain coursed through my temples and down my neck. Slumping to the floor, I squeezed my eyes shut and prayed for the pain to go away. Excruciating pressure in my temples sent waves of nausea through me. The room spun wildly. Someone was twisting knives into the sides of my head. Fierce ringing in my ears convinced me that my head was about to explode. Certain I was having a stroke, writhing in pain, I welcomed death. But gradually the pain subsided. I opened my eyes slowly, knowing with absolute certainty that the ravishing red cardinal was the last thing I would ever see. Where before I'd been in a gray-black world, what took its place was a blinding snowstorm, the total whiteout I now inhabit.

I had traded my world of darkness for a world of too much light. The pain in my head still comes and goes, but it is never as severe as it was that morning in the kitchen. What I see is like the static on a black-and-white television when there is poor reception. If someone or something comes within eight inches of my nose and is backlit, I might see a faint shadow. But since I can't make out what the shadow is, I find it more startling than informative. Bright light, just normal daylight, can bring on the crackling pain of a migraine headache. When I go outside, or into my studio to work, I have to put on dark glasses for protection.

It felt like my life had been reduced to the level of mold. Mold thrives in darkness, in damp cellars, tenacious and nonproductive. I wondered obsessively about the purpose of my existence. Here I was, a throbbing blob of consciousness breathing in and out, a body disconnected from its native habitat. There was no escaping the deafening sound of my breathing, the sensation of blood coursing through my veins. I ate and slept and felt the glacial passing of every moment. But what was the point? I pondered life's existential questions. Why am I here? Why bother? Is there more to life than just breathing? What could possibly give meaning to my life? Will I just go on, day after day after day, without purpose or goals, like a vegetable, until my stagnating brain comes to a stop? Is it enough to get up in the morning, find my way to the kitchen, and drink a cup of coffee? *I don't think so.*

Al was improving rapidly. His ability to speak was more or less back to normal. When he couldn't find the right words or had trouble cobbling together a sentence, he resorted to a tolerable level of profanity. He still had some short-term memory deficits, and his math abilities had come to rest at about a third-grade level. Drugs now stabilized his mood swings. Al was feeling much better and was, in essential ways, back in charge of his own life. I, on the other hand, had no work and no friends and was pretty much confined to quarters, except at Al's whim. I was no longer Al's caretaker, the role to which I'd devoted myself for the past year. I was reduced to taking in enough air to sustain life.

It seemed that things could not get worse. But I was wrong. Just at this juncture my precious Nova suddenly went into seizures and I had to have her put down. For fourteen years, Nova had been my constant companion, the perfect friend and confidante for someone who didn't have friends in whom to confide. Nova offered me the unconditional love and companionship that I couldn't trust people to give me. She kept my innermost secrets, and was always there to comfort me and share my grief. She was happy with everything we did. Years later I realized that Nova taught me the meaning of life. She lived in the moment.

Losing Nova was more than I could bear. Hazy roiling images, in macabre shades of gray, of Nova hemorrhaging on the kitchen floor played like a continuous tape loop in my mind's eye. In a frenzy of grief and rage, I found the keys to my Honda, which had been patiently waiting for my eyesight to return. Guided by bright lights and looming shadows, fueled by floods of grief, I drove to a nearby motel in the middle of the night. I suppose I was seeking a passive exit from my hopeless life. Why I didn't total the car or injure someone, I will never know. I hoped that I would take my last breath in that room. Al, ever my knight in shining armor, found me crumpled in the middle of the king-size bed in my motel room and brought me home. But this was the end for me. My life was over. I crawled back to bed and waited to die. All I wanted was sweet oblivion, but I was too depressed even to muster the initiative to commit suicide.

Weeks passed. Under the covers in the dark, I could barely breathe. Fine. Who needed to breathe? Al was furious that I wasn't doing anything. *Like what? Driving to the market and picking up dinner?* I hated where we were living, out in the suburbs, where I had none of the freedom and mobility I'd had at the hospital in San Diego. Georgetown, Texas, had no public transportation, not even a taxi service. In our neighborhood the houses were acres apart. It was a community of commuters who left early every morning and drove to Austin. Isolation and silence surrounded me day after day, week after week, reinforcing my feeling of being lost in infinity.

I hated that Al could come and go as he pleased, while I was again totally dependent on him. He could not comprehend that I had no goals, no desire to be productive, that I just did not care about anything or anyone. I was beyond emotional and physical exhaustion, and I knew that I would never recover. Al kept pressuring me to gain some independence, urging me to come up with a wish list of what I wanted to do with my life. He used every ploy he could think of to get me out of bed. Refusing to feed me had no effect, so sometimes he'd give in and bring me something to eat or drink, or try to trick me into going to a class. But I wasn't having any of this, and I fought him at every turn. He was at the end of his already shortened rope. "Either we can do this together," he threatened, "or I can leave you here." He stopped responding to my calls for help, and I stopped calling.

One day, Al came into our bedroom, switched on the lights, and threw a set of child's watercolors and a drawing tablet on top of my comforter.

"You've got to do something," he snapped. "Why don't you try a little art therapy?"

I was speechless. Livid! Stunned! I threw them back at him as he ducked out the door. "I can't see, in case you hadn't noticed. How dare you, how could you be so insensitive?"

My heart was in my throat, my mind was racing. Breathing so hard I could have had my own heart attack, I groped, with the paints and pad, to the desk in the hall. In the bright light, with the hazy narrow band of central vision remaining to me, I could just make out the shape of a squat round jar on the hall shelf. In five minutes I dashed off a row of repeating jars just like it, one overlapping the other, each time stabbing my brush into a different color, colors I could no longer see. "Is this red, or green?" I ranted.

"There's your goddamn painting," I screamed to the empty room. "I hope you're satisfied." My anger could have charred the paper. "What do you want from me? Your wife is blind, damn it." With each brushstroke, I cursed louder. "What do you expect? I can't see!" Suddenly spent, I threw the painting on the floor and crawled back to my bed.

PART II

REGROUP

CHAPTER FOUR

FIRST LIGHT

A work of art is the trace of a magnificent struggle.

—ROBERT HENRI

NOW IT WAS DECREED that I become a painter. Al, and everyone he showed it to, declared the *Jars* painting a miracle. Learning to paint was the obvious answer to my predicament. My eager caretakers signed me up for a two-week class at an art school in Ruston, Louisiana, where, in case I needed help, there was a nearby school for the blind. I would learn to paint and have a life beyond my twelve-by-sixteen-foot room. I would return whole, an artist. My friend Linda agreed with Al that my "marvel" of a painting was some kind of sign. She decided to accompany me to Ruston and take the class too. Linda and Al meant well, but I couldn't help feeling that their enthusiasm was motivated by a desire to solve their own predicament: me.

I had no interest in art or art classes. I had no desire to leave my bed. Indifferent to all the fuss, I stayed under the covers. As I came to grips with the permanent reversal of my eyesight and accepted the futility of further surgeries, my depression darkened. Fearing for my hopeless mind-set, my devoted social worker, Susan, pushed for immediate enrollment at the Criss Cole Rehabilitation Center in Austin, Texas, not banishment to Ruston.

Al believed that a stint at an art school, maybe another few weeks to settle into a routine at home, and my rehabilitation would be complete. He admitted that he was not prepared to be alone for the months of separation that formal rehabilitation would require. Al was convinced that Susan was exaggerating my problems. He could not fathom why I was having such difficulty adjusting.

Linda made valiant efforts to engage me in finger painting, in the wonders of art, in the joy of working in clay. *No thanks. In case you haven't noticed, I can't see and I don't care.* As our departure date drew near, Linda saw the limits of my mobility and motivation, and chickened out. "That painting was just a fluke," she decided. "I don't want the responsibility for the safety of someone blind." She felt Al had done a marvelous job with my rehabilitation. It was enough that I was again eating, sleeping, and responding to questions.

Just when Al and Linda recognized the folly of their scheme, I suddenly saw this art class as a chance to escape my misery. I insisted on going to Ruston, alone. *If I can't escape life by driving off the expressway, maybe I can escape it by getting lost in Louisiana.* Al packed my bags and off we went to Ruston. Our new pound pooch, Wizard, was quietly attentive in the back seat. Someone should have filmed that drive: the driver who forgot where he was going every few miles, and his blind sidekick with the photographic memory.

Driver: "We're at the Ninden exit on I-20 heading east. Now what?"

Sidekick: "Get back on the freeway and go another fifty miles, to Exit 67. Then go three lights and make a left."

We got lost only once. (On the way home, with Wizard in the passenger seat, Al called me to check in every two hours, but he still got sidetracked four times. When he finally reached the house, Al called and said he was shocked to see our drive-way, and he turned to Wizard to ask him if it really was our home.)

In my room at Ruston, Al helped me unpack and oriented me to the space. He labeled the closets, doors, drawers, and lights with Braille markers, quizzing me incessantly about the layout of my room and surroundings. He made certain I could locate the telephone on the wall and dial our home number correctly. Finally, he hugged me good-bye.

Good riddance. I wasn't there to study art. I had no interest in painting. I was here to escape from Al, and from everyone's expectations. To be left alone with my depression. I expected two hassle-free weeks. No one to wake me up, no one to prod me to eat, no one hovering over me expecting a smile.

I also anticipated a new freedom at Ruston. No one there had known me pre-blindness, so I could be anyone I wanted to be. I would be treated just like one of the group. The idea of not only learning to live with blindness but returning to Al as a new person was very appealing, very liberating. I was deter-mined to change and adapt. The part of me that wasn't plan-ning to sleep all day, the part of me that wasn't afraid that I would fail, wanted desperately to learn to live in the world of the sighted, as Susan had so often exhorted me to do. I would learn to mimic normal behavior, to judge distances properly and replace sight with logic. *Yes, I can.*

I was exhilarated—for about ten minutes, until the utter mystery of my surroundings hit me. I sat stiffly on my bed, afraid to make the slightest move. When my roommate arrived, I could feel my shoulders relax and my breathing return to nor-mal. She sailed into the room, tossing her suitcase and art sup-plies on her bed. "I'm exhausted," she said, turning to me, "so why don't you help me unpack that suitcase and I'll do this one." In the next moment she saw my cane and let out a little yelp.

"You're blind, how can that be?" No one, it seems, had warned her. She was so incensed by the idea that she was supposed to "babysit" someone blind that she went marching down the hall to find "someone in charge." She hadn't asked my name or given me hers, but she was already certain I was a loser. When she discovered that no one was available to respond to her questions and I was not able to help her unpack, she was livid. Her first act of aggression was to tear off Al's carefully placed Braille markers. I tried to reason with her, but she declared that the situation was impossible. She had a point, but I was in desperate straits. While we yelled at each other, she rearranged the furniture to accommodate her sense of *balance*.

My roommate's grumbling never let up. When I tripped over her trunk and bloodied my nose, she took the incident as proof that I had no right to be taking a painting course. Fortunately, a kind woman from across the hall broke up our shouting match, escorted me to the bathroom, and promised to help me get to class the next day.

By bedtime my roommate and I had declared a truce. It was now well after midnight, and I was tired and thoroughly confused. I tossed and turned through the night in a strange room in a strange land where I could barely find my pillow and had no idea of the whereabouts of my clothes or hairbrush. With no way to tell the time, I was hypervigilant, alert to every sound in the hall, worried that my new friend, Mae, would forget to wake me and lead me to class. Helpless as I was, I resented being so dependent, telling myself that soon I wouldn't need her.

Mae came for me as promised, led me to the bathroom, and helped me find something to wear. It's awful not to know if your blouse is on straight, to suspect that you look ridiculous and no one will tell you. I certainly wasn't going to ask. Everything was moving so fast—on sighted people's time. I could never stand still long enough to get my bearings, could barely wash my face. A shower was out of the question. I was propelled across a featureless landscape—lawn, sidewalks, up and down stairs, curbs, and into a mystery building with endless halls—to a high stool at a table.

Exhausted and thoroughly disoriented, I sat on the stool, trying to catch my breath and calm myself. What had I been thinking? Why hadn't I asked for a floor plan in advance? Why hadn't I prepared? Even as I struggled to take deep breaths, I browbeat myself. *Where is my brain? Just because I can't see, am I also brain-dead?*

Under the constant overload of learning to manage the world, you are in a fog so thick that you cannot think. It is not exactly dread or fear; it feels more like a nightmare of suffocation. You are awake in this nightmare, and you are alone in a dark room. An invisible force presses on your lungs. You can barely take a full breath, and your limbs are so heavy they ache. Suddenly a dark shadow startles you, and you feel like someone has dumped ice water over your naked body. You awake in an alien land, freezing.

So here I was shivering on this stool, trying to be invisible and feeling very much a fool. Being blind was no excuse for not even having considered that the information I sorely needed might have been in the registration package. In an agony of recrimination and general affliction, a feeling of foreboding came over me when I realized that this was *not* a nightmare. *This is my life; there is no way out.* My hands and feet began to perspire, and all the smells in the room (body odor and perfume, paint and solvents) washed over me in a malodorous smog. A sharp metallic tang on my tongue produced cold sweat and nausea. I was barely holding it together. I began to have palpitations, and I was consumed with the desire to run. Running is what I've done all my life. It occurred to me how ironic it was that blindness, of all maladies, had chosen me, and now rooted me to this precarious stool that I clung to for dear life. My sense of paralysis intensified.

All of this was occurring in slow motion. It felt as if I had been sitting on that stool in hell for years, although it had been but a minute. Then my hearing kicked in through the fog, and the babble, din, jangle, and clatter of thirty eager women setting up shop crashed over me. *Oh yes.* I am here in Ruston, Louisiana, in a loud, smelly, scary real-life hell. I must focus. I must learn the rules and parameters of this reality.

When you can see, you are not as susceptible to such acute sensory distortion, nor is it such a struggle to right yourself. You open your eyes and refocus, and the experience of being overwhelmed dissipates. When you are blind, establishing and maintaining the world's solidity is a perpetual task for the mind, not the eye, a cerebral challenge. You try to hold a mental picture of your surroundings—insofar as you can construct them—firmly in mind. You count steps, remember left and right turns. You know how far to reach for the light switch. When you are blind, your reality is that the nightmare is always waiting to take hold. You must learn to instantly determine if approaching footsteps signal friend or foe. Defenseless in your dark world, you always first imagine that the sound portends harm. This irrational reaction, born of your sense of being powerless to respond, makes you feel like you've been sucker punched in the gut, knocking the breath out of you. I frequently had the uncontrollable impulse to "glance up" to be sure that everything was all right, to ensure that my initial fright was unfounded. But I was a scared and defenseless blind person, wholly at the mercy of the strangers whose breath and scent surrounded me.

―――――――――――

Okay, so I was sitting at a table in the back of the room that Al and I had briefly reconnoitered the day before. Immediately I discovered what a bad choice we'd made. Ever since that migraine attack in April, when my inner darkness gave way to snow-blind whiteness, bright light has been my nemesis. The light streaming in the bank of windows running along the wall to my left stabbed my eyes like daggers. Yesterday the space had been empty and so quiet you could hear the hum of the fluorescent lights. Today it was bedlam. The collective noise of chattering students and their radios, the scraping of tables and chairs being moved around, and the ever-changing obstacle course of objects in the aisles created havoc with my bearings. My tinted glasses barely controlled the psychedelic play of light bouncing off the Formica tabletops, the painting trays, the walls and ceilings. In this disorienting hall of mirrors, ghost bodies moved all around me in a continual dance. There was no way to bring the space to order.

The helpful Mae had literally plopped me in place. "Don't move," she'd admonished. "I'll be right back." In a desperate attempt to drown out the noise and my beating heart, I shut down. I pretended I was home, safe under my comforters.

―――――――――――

"So where are your tools? Where are your paints and paper?" Returning an hour later, Mae was astonished that I wasn't set up to work. Well, I did not have any tools, since I hadn't read the list of things needed for the first day of class. The class, as it turned out, was designed for experienced painters, not a novice. It was to be a "watercolor encounter" class with an emphasis on self-expression. The idea was to approach painting from a new perspective, to unleash the inner creative self and regain one's creative edge. The other students had been painting, some at a professional level, for years. They knew, for instance, that "watercolor encounter" referred not to just the medium of transparent watercolors but, rather, to any medium soluble in water. They had a comprehension of art terminology and the principles of art. Many had attended the teacher's prior workshops and knew their way around the studio and grounds. They came prepared with supplies and tools. They were ready to work, unlike me, who just wanted to get away. And they could see.

So I just sat there and listened to the teacher talk about images I couldn't see, and perform demonstrations that I had no way of following, as tears streamed down my face. Someone on my right forced a box of Kleenex into my hand. "Honey, it only gets worse," she said. "I've taken this class before and it's a bear."

It is not always easy to tell that someone is blind. My clear green eyes look normal. I am not in a wheelchair, and as usual I was hiding my cane. I was trying so hard to keep it together. My mother had taught me that tears made me vulnerable, and that vulnerability made me a victim. Letting other people see my pain or tears was not in my repertoire. This woman assumed that I was overwhelmed by the class outline. My problem was the fear that I was coming unglued, coupled with the impossibility of escape. I could not go home, back to Al and the shaky ground of our constant squabbling. I could not let others see I'd failed. I had no choice but to stick it out, to somehow keep it together and get through this experience, so I could go back home and bury myself under the covers again. And sleep.

But the noise, the noise. I could not get a solid sense of where I was; by now even my sense of *who* I was seemed to be slipping away. I had been so accustomed to quiet. No radio, no TV, no people sounds. Here it was like being on an airport runway, with sound coming from all directions: under my feet the shuffling of boxes and footsteps; at waist level people sliding, scraping, *arranging;* the buzz of human conversations quiet and loud, jabbering groups, coughing; dueling radio stations, water running; and no way, absolutely no way, to distinguish what was imminent and what was not. I was in a fever pitch of sensory overload.

I quickly discovered that before I could even think about my art education, I needed to reduce, detail by detail, my feeling of complete helplessness, first and foremost by mastering the space. Memorizing the classroom layout was my initial lesson. I learned to make sweeping exploratory motions with my arms to determine width, length, and height. This you do one location at a time, then one object at a time. You start by locating with hands, feet, and cane the large objects (desk, stool, wall) and then reconnoiter the small items (brushes, erasers, pencils, paper). Then you hope and pray that *nothing* will move. Getting a sense of a complex space entails establishing the position of one object and connecting it to the next, and the next, calculating the spaces in between as you go, and then repeating the process over and over for verification. Finally you commit your mental construct to memory. It's a painstaking additive process, one you repeat thousands of times a day, every day. The sighted take in everything at once, editing and prioritizing their visual field, quickly eliminating irrelevant objects and information to distinguish what is of value to them. It's a no-brainer subtractive process, performed flawlessly and automatically by the teamwork of mind and eye.

Ever so slowly in the ensuing days I made my way in this new world. I entered the classroom through a wide door into a room with windows along the entire left wall of the space. There were three rows of ten worktables, each six feet long by about three feet deep, set about four feet apart. I sat on a high stool at a chest-high table. There was a wall to my right, which halfway along its length opened into another cavernous studio. At the far end of that room was a door leading into the lecture and demonstration area, at the front of which was the instructor's chair and desk, with a blackboard and some kind of corkboard along the back wall. Facing the instructor's desk were rows six across and five deep of individual student desks, the kind with the writing table attached on the right to an old-fashioned wood and metal base. Directly to the right of this space was an area of similar size that housed sinks, paint-mixing units, and light tables around the outer walls. In the center of that space a twelve-by-eight-foot table was piled with "stuff"—junk, found objects, visually interesting items to use in still-life compositions, as though someone had dumped out the detritus from the archaeology museum archives. From this haphazard pile students chose objects of interest to set up a tableau they'd then paint.

I'm boring you, perhaps, but I could go on in far greater detail. When I talk to former classmates, they have scant recall of the layout of this space that I now know by heart. This information is immediately available to them again on sight or in a photograph. They have no need to file such data in their memories.

———————————

Then there was the art-making itself. The paraphernalia needed to create a single piece of art—masonite or board, paints and pencils of the desired colors, palette knife, water in a container, clips, brushes, erasers, textured mediums, and paper towels, not to mention an idea that matched the day's assignment—felt like another mountain to climb.

The notion that I could pull all this together to paint was ludicrous. The first day our genial teacher, Doug Walton, did a "Hello, has everyone here got their art supplies?" introduction. *Well, no, as a matter of fact, I wasn't actually planning on painting. Can't you see I'm blind?* Off I went to the campus art supply store with my compliant dorm mates to buy the required materials. I spent the first three days of class just trying to get my gear in order so that I could locate what I needed.

Now it seems hilarious, but I had the hardest time keeping my brushes from rolling off the slightly slanted worktable. I was too discombobulated to solve the problem simply by putting them in a container. I repeatedly placed them on the desk, heard them roll off, then crawled around on my hands and knees searching for them, trying to hold back my tears. I repeated this exercise several times each day, until Mae brought me a jar for the brushes. Then all I had to do was learn not to tip over the jar.

Each morning's routine began with a motivational lecture from Doug about creativity or self-expression, followed by an art lesson. This might be a talk about color theory or composition, perspective or edges. I taped his lectures so that I could review them at home when I wasn't so distraught and distracted, and I taped my own notes as well. Next he would critique the prior day's work. I had no work. My job was not to knock anything over in the middle of class.

Then the class moved into action, warming up with a timed ten- to thirty-minute quickie exercise designed to engage the more intuitive right side of the brain. Brush warm-ups were about learning to express yourself, and this was intended as free-play time. But it seemed that most everyone was focused on the finished product, not the journey of self-discovery. When the timer was started, the horde of artists stampeded to create a finished painting from a still life Doug had assembled. It was a competition that I could not join; at this point a viable painting was out of the question for me.

Although Doug fully supported my participation in the class, despite the gibes and grumbling of those who resented my presence or insisted that it was "impossible" for a blind person to paint, I was overwhelmed. How was I supposed to complete an assignment to "paint the statue on the table in relation to the bottle of water on your desk" when I had trouble buttoning my blouse? How was I to understand foreshortening or perspective in the visually oriented language he used to explain it? Everything in my world was one-dimensional; I had no reference for distance or perspective. I could touch the water bottle, hold it in my hand, but that statue out there in the ether? I hadn't a clue.

After our lunch break Doug gave us an assignment for the next day, which we spent the remainder of the afternoon developing. The procedure was to draw your composition on lightweight white poster paper and perfect the design in stages, recopying it at each stage onto other pieces of poster paper, using a light box to trace the image. When you were satisfied with the composition, you went back to the light box. A sheet of quality watercolor paper was then superimposed on top of your design, allowing you to trace an outline of the image with black acrylic paint. Your final painting was then done, in preparation for the next day's critique. *Repositioning and recopying? In my dreams.*

The class worked in this highly competitive stew from one in the afternoon until about ten at night, returning to class at nine the next morning for more of the same. The thoughtful Doug, concerned that I could not use the light boxes or the acrylic tracing technique, assigned everyone painting partners. It was a kind gesture, in theory, but not a practical one. I was far from able to use paint without getting it all over me, as well as every surface or person I touched. The painting-partner arrangement raised to a higher level what had been a subdued level of grumbling about special treatment for me. I was not shunned, but the posse of detractors that my irascible roommate had rallied around her grew.

I spent the first week learning to maneuver around my dorm room, my roommate, and my art supplies. My roommate told everyone I "could not possibly" be blind. Like many people, she assumed that blindness meant you see nothing, that the world of the blind is pitch-black. I tried to explain that blindness covers a range of visual impairments, but she was determined to unmask my "scam." She would leave a chair in the middle of the room, and sure enough, I'd fall over it. I'd cut myself on an X-Acto knife left unsheathed on a table. She would leave a wet towel or painting on my bed and get angry when I sat on them or dropped them to the floor. She left me notes I could not read and confirmed appointments that, in my ignorance, I did not keep. I'd scream at her and she would scream at me. We did not act like adults. She baited me with taunts that I would never be an artist.

Maybe not, but I was determined to try. I was so thrilled with my first painting, five days into the class, that I could hardly wait for Doug's critique. My image was to be a billowing peacock feather spilling over the edges of the paper, in brilliant blues and greens, with highlights of violet and yellow. For two hours I worked to get the paint consistency right, not too runny or too dry. My imagination raced ahead as I carefully drew the lines in black acrylic paint. Patiently I used a hair dryer to speed the drying time. Afraid I would miss a spot on the twenty-two-by-thirty-inch watercolor paper (it seemed like a huge expanse to me), I placed a ruler horizontally across the sheet, moving it down the paper in tiny increments to guide each brushstroke. Other students left for dinner and returned as I diligently applied color to every vein, shaft, and plume of my drawing, running my fingers over each faint line to orient myself. I wanted that peacock feather to jump off the page. Six hours later, covered in paint, having used every one of my new brushes, I was elated. I thought I had tossed off an original masterpiece, only to discover that I had painted the whole thing in one color. Blue. So much for my fledgling brilliance.

Clearly I was going to need more refined discernment skills. Doug's support was unflagging. When I'd whine that I couldn't see the colors or the paper, he'd say, "So just paint," the best possible advice. Doug's basic strategy was to encourage me to simply keep trying, which at the time I didn't fully appreciate. His class did not teach me to paint, but his caring support touched me on a deeper level.

As the days passed, my ability to use the tools and to take my chances on the outcome improved. Doug began to hold me up as an example of tapping into one's creative courage. Every day he'd have some comment: "At least Lisa tried to finish the exercise" or "Lisa's progress is inspiring." This royally irritated the other students, who were sick of hearing about the blind paragon of virtue. While I welcomed Doug's support, it intensified my sense of alienation and the animosity of the cadre that wanted me gone. They felt that the support I was getting was unfounded and that it was unfair to take time from the regular classroom instruction to give me the individual attention I required. I suppose it was. The resentment was also a wake-up call for me to recognize that not everyone was thrilled or impressed that I wanted to paint.

I had to face the fact that I could not learn art in the usual way, in classes where the instruction was steeped in visual terminology, where techniques were illustrated by demonstrations or slide shows. The language of art, based on visual perception, is almost impenetrable to a blind person. I would have to find my own way, my own system and cosmology of art. I was beginning to understand that what the mind loses when sight is gone must be re-created through other means. I would have to adapt my perceptual palette to my new circumstances, and find alternative ways of understanding the principles of line, contour, and perspective.

But first I would have to raise my ability to get from the dorm to the classroom, and to handle other basics of daily life, to a far higher level. My dorm mates escorted me to class each day, taking me by the hand, prodding me from behind, or grabbing my clothes. Off balance and without any point of reference to orient myself, I could barely construct some sense of where I was going. On the fourth day, without mentioning it, they took a new route to class. I was following along with my cane as best I could when my guide's attention was distracted by someone calling her name. This is a normal reaction for a sighted person, but an unforgivable lapse if you are leading the blind. I tumbled down three stone steps and into a shallow pond. I emerged drenched and bruised, forcing all of us back to the dorm to deal with my predicament, and making all of us late for class. If I'd had navigational skills, the swimming lesson would have been avoided. At the very least, I could have returned to the dorm independently. Well, they got their own lesson about giving me specific verbal directions, and they began to draw straws over who would be responsible for me each day.

After several days without bathing, I worked up my courage to shower in the dorm bathroom. Having groped my way to a shower stall, I had no idea which tap was hot and which was cold water, or for that matter how to turn on the faucet. For what felt like an ice age, I stood naked in the cold echo chamber, a grid of goose bumps rising on my skin, unable to find a place to put the shampoo, with no clue where the water would come out. Here I was again, paralyzed by the impenetrability of my surroundings, when someone reached across me wordlessly and turned on the water.

"At least I won't have to share a space with a pig." The unmistakable drawl of my roommate sent new shivers up my spine. With no directions as to how to shut the water off or regulate the temperature, she left me in a cascade of freezing spray. Someone with her wits about her would have stepped out of the shower and asked for instructions. But I was blind and witless. Finally I yelled for help. A voice called out that I should rotate the dial about three inches to my left for hotter water and push the faucet handle in and down to shut the water off. Well, I turned the faucet but overcorrected to scalding water. I leapt from the shower in a panic, sprawling onto a bathroom floor made slick by my flood. Someone shoved a towel into my hands. When I caught my breath, I was mortified.

The first time I went to the cafeteria, I tried to pour myself a glass of ice water from a dispenser. People to my left and right were perfectly willing to do it for me, but how hard could it be to fill a glass with water? Initially the machine baffled me, but after several false starts I found the release button on the spout.

Not until I heard yelling did I realize that I'd overfilled my glass and sprayed the whole area with cold water. Back at the table, I reached to drink from my full glass and toppled it onto someone's lap. Having apologized profusely, I managed to dispense another glass of water and set it on the table. But I placed the glass too far away and ended up drinking someone else's iced tea. Over the course of two weeks, through a succession of wet people and apologies, I got the hang of getting a glass of water and setting it on the table where I could find it. But by then my classmates' patience with my ineptitude was fast fading.

I kept thinking that if I could just bring the chaos under control a bit, calm down, and get my bearings, I could better manage my situation. I could ask for what I needed in clear and specific terms, rather than having to accept the well-meaning but ill-considered help I was typically getting.

"Don't just nod or point when I ask directions," I wanted to tell them. "I can't see your body language." "Don't just grab my arm. It startles me and throws me off balance; just touch me lightly under the elbow so I can put my hand on your shoulder or follow your voice." "Please don't push me from behind." "Always describe to me where we are going, and the terrain along the way. Are we coming to a stairway? How long will we be walking across this lawn? Are we going to turn?"

I sought cooperation, negotiation, détente, but this was rare. Most sighted people assumed they knew what I needed. Some people would edit information and make decisions, rather than asking my view or preference. When I specified what I wanted or escalated my demands, they felt I was ungrateful for their help. Others' information was imprecise, risky, or inaccurate. They had no frame of reference for the kind of complete information I required, data that the sighted take for granted. This is why, in the days before I knew the right way to ask for help, I often ended up in the men's room.

I was exhausted with the effort of trying to keep up. My sight was gone, forever. No one was going to wait for me to analyze the number of steps to the sink or a wall. Life went on around me, and I had to learn to do more than dress myself to survive. I did not have the luxury of calmly assessing which aspects of visual perception I needed to regain. Time did not permit me to draw up a plan of action, as I would have done in my sighted life. At times it was all I could do to muster the patience and mental energy required to move from my desk to the sink. Everyone is most comfortable in familiar surroundings, especially the blind. But the blind are almost always in unfamiliar territory. I can remember being in the dorm or the studio or the cafeteria, thinking, "I need to wake up. I am not problem solving." My mind was exhausted. Conversations would be buzzing around me and I would be obsessing about how I could paint the water bottle in the context of the statue on the pedestal.

"Find the object's essence," Doug kept saying. But to order my life, I had to take the opposite approach. I was living in the essence. My task was to find the context, to cobble together a workable reality from the pieces I could access through my remaining senses. When you are blind there is no "reality." You have to make it up as you go, and hope that your version of reality is relevant. I needed to break down the tasks I performed daily into discrete learning units. I needed to ramp up my mental mapping skills.

A person who is visually impaired or blind creates a master mental map of every situation, using whatever information he can gather—visual memories, reports from the sighted, written material, sounds, smells, objects within reach—before taking the first step. Before I make a move, I need to know exactly where I am. Then I establish where I want to be and come up with a plan to cover the distance in between. Like the sighted, I try to anticipate my route, and to avoid obstacles that might cause a collision. I conserve energy by mentally choosing the most direct route, and I time my travel to meet a schedule. But unlike the sighted, I perform a mental test run before entering and exiting every space. I am like the Olympic skiers you see on television, silently gyrating through the course in a mental practice run as they await the start of a race. The sighted also experience anxiety and tension when navigating in new situations or unfamiliar places (airports, office buildings, busy city streets). But this anxiety arises from having insufficient time to process visual information, not from a lack of information to process. I spend a great deal of energy collecting information.

When Al called each night to inquire how the art was going, I wanted to scream my frustration. *I'm not painting! It's all I can do to find the classroom.* The more solicitous he was, the stronger my impulse to slam the receiver in his ear. Al was counting on getting a functional wife back. He was in for a big surprise.

Looking back on my Ruston adventure, it is clear to me that I wasn't in my right mind. I was in no position to deal calmly and courteously with all that was happening to me. There was no logic to attending an art school for the sighted and expecting others to accommodate me. Truly I was lost in space, stranded far outside my comfort zone, exhausted by the vigilance called for every step of the way. But Ruston was a turning point. However badly I was handling myself, however erratically I was being helped or hindered, I was in fact learning to function on my own. I began, for the first time in my long siege, to have moments of internal calm. I no longer jumped at every sound, was no longer embarrassed because I couldn't see an object in my path, no longer expected tasks to be easily accomplished. I was learning to ask for what I wanted in a clear and forceful manner, without the edge of angry defensiveness that often laced my requests.

For so long I had been too afraid and uncomfortable to consider doing anything more complex than breathing. At Ruston I found the multisensory stimulation, as important to my survival as water, that my brain needed to stay alive. I discovered that there were perceptual tools that, if I mastered them, could widen my world and make it manageable. Most of all, I was beginning to recognize that in art I had found my life's passion, the path that would lead me back into the world. I guess Al knew what he was doing when he bought me that watercolor set and packed me off to painting school.

At the end of a seemingly interminable two weeks, Al returned with Wizard and a huge bouquet of daylilies. "So what have you painted?" he asked once we were settled in the car.

I broke out in wrenching sobs. "Well, I bought some cool supplies, brushes and paints and paper. I made two new friends, and I learned to trust my judgment again. I'm learning to get around on my own. I think I can learn to paint. So I have signed up for two more weeks, and we'll be coming back again in August." I slumped in my seat, still sobbing. Wizard climbed into my lap, and I welcomed his warmth. I was beyond exhaustion. But there was no stopping me now.

CHAPTER FIVE

WALKING IN SPACE

*One can have no smaller or greater mastery
than mastery of oneself.*

—LEONARDO DA VINCI

I OFFICIALLY ACCEPTED MY BLINDNESS in Ruston, Louisiana, in June 1995, not the day I was labeled "legally blind" or after my failed surgery, when all hope for a cure died. Ruston One, as I refer to those first two weeks of little art and lots of fumbling around in the dark, represents for me the period when I stopped talking about what it is like to be blind and just began to live it. Heeding Susan's voice in my ear, I began to analyze what was required for a blind person to live in a sighted world. Of course, when Susan talked about choosing a life in the sighted world, she meant one a little more conventional than the one I presently live. Still, now I knew that there were norms of behavior, roles, and expectations that made blindness more palatable. There was a guidebook for being blind, and all I needed to do was to memorize its contents.

Knowing that there were tested methods for getting from Point A to Point B helped me to gain independence, even if I ended up doing things my own way. I'd always been a visual learner. With my photographic memory, I could reiterate verbatim anything I'd read. As a financial analyst, I'd astounded my colleagues with my ability to quote fluctuating stock prices, commodities trades, and currency differentials over weeks and months of trading. Now I needed to call on my powers of memory and concentration, my organizational and analytical skills, and my life experience to aid me in replacing what I'd lost.

The scariest thing about being blind is that the world is an illusion. Until you make it concrete, bit by bit, you are at the mercy of your demons. Unless you keep your mind stimulated, unless you constantly verify the world out there, you are prone to fantasy and distortions. You must hold off the terror, lest it overwhelm you. To do that, I painstakingly populate my mind with the images I remember. I am always on guard to keep reality and fantasy separate. To constantly revalidate an object's reality takes huge stores of emotional energy.

Intellectually I understand the three-dimensionality of phenomena, but I live in a flat, one-pointed universe. Without sight, my ability to create a mental image of a three-dimensional space is severely challenged. Unless I make the effort to "dimensionalize" them, the people, places, animals, and objects I recall now look more like the paper dolls I played with as a child, without depth or color. Through continuous concentrated remembering, I keep alive details of their outlines, contours, and hue, and I use these memories to reconstruct the world. It was up to me to create my own real-time virtual reality. Quite simply, I had to become the programmer of my own 3-D video game. Constructing small worlds with paint on paper would help me navigate the three-dimensional world. Honing my sense of hearing, touch, and smell would expand my reach.

I was a whirlwind of activity during the six weeks between sessions at Ruston. At last I was motivated to join the world of the living. I mean the *sighted*. Now I lamented my months in bed, in the dark. I was desperate to make up for lost time, greedy for new skills. Every new task was a welcome challenge. I practiced putting my clothes in the washing machine and starting it up, over and over and over, until I got it right and there was no spilled detergent and no odd item of clothing dropped on the floor. I walked alone in my own backyard for the first time, circumnavigating the same live oak tree, using my trusty cane. When I tripped or bumped into things, it was of no matter to me. Finally I was willing to take chances, to fail, to fall down, to repeat the simplest action an infinite number of times until I got it right.

I made a detailed list of the tasks I wanted to master, broken down into their tiniest components. I would learn to make a salad, to iron my clothes, to walk to the dry cleaner's. I crammed the six weeks with drills, exercises, and forays into uncharted territory—like the nearest street corner, chair, or revolving door. If you think making a peanut butter and jelly sandwich is easy, you are mistaken. It is a journey of a thousand steps. Try it sometime blindfolded. I listened, over and over, to the tapes I'd made of Doug's lectures and reviewed my notes, to be sure I was ready for the next round of classes.

We returned to Ruston in early August, with a mountain of new art supplies and a new skill set I was eager to test out. I had elected to bunk solo this time around. Al once again ordered my space and labeled the drawers and desk. He walked me to the cafeteria, gave me a complete tour of the classroom and bathroom. He reviewed the bathroom fixtures and put me through the shower drill. We located the ATM machine, icemaker, and telephones. He alerted me to hazardous curbs and stairs as we walked the campus. This time around, I was determined not to be a burden for my dorm mates. My goal was to learn more about art, about myself, and about independence. I wanted to participate in the class as an artist, to lose myself in the art-making process.

Art, I knew, was my salvation. I believed that if I could learn to paint according to the principles of art, I would learn to "see" again and the world would return to normal. If I could apply the basic concepts of art to canvas, I could reconstruct my world. Already I was imagining in detail that statue "out there." I did not want to paint abstracts, which I'd been told were all I could hope for. I wanted to learn to paint shape and form. I wanted to learn to paint *reality.*

I expected the class I signed up for to be a repeat of my first two weeks in Ruston, except that this time I might actually learn something about how to paint. *Wrong again.* "No," Doug informed me. "This class is about design and color theory, not about creativity."

Okay, fine. Maybe it was more important for me to understand the concepts of visual perception than to produce art. See how adaptable I was becoming? I had already painted my all-blue fiasco. Maybe it was better that I didn't paint. Art theory was the doorway into my ability to retake the world. Intellectually breaking down the logistics of producing art on a small scale would enable me to find my way in the big unwieldy world in which I lurched around like a drunken sailor.

Doug laughed at my blithe arrogance. "Researchers have spent lifetimes learning just how people understand visual objects and employ them in everyday living. You're not exactly inventing the wheel." But he agreed that my goal of mastering the principals of art was a good one.

"After all," he said in passing, "there is little chance that you can learn to paint shape and form."

———————————

Toppling over furniture, ending up in the wrong bathroom, spilling cold water on my friends, and dressing in mismatched clothes had prompted me to tackle spatial relationships, the topic of one of Doug's lectures. I didn't have a concrete definition of the term, but I understood it as the ability to order and interpret physical phenomena.

Spatial awareness permits the brain to process complex elements simultaneously: direction, depth perception, form constancy, the position of objects in a given space, and visual integration along vertical, horizontal, and diagonal planes. This complex awareness is in play every time you pass through a door, step off a curb, pull a sweater over your head, or pick up a book. Analyzing yet another process that I'd performed automatically for so many years, I was amazed at the brain's ability to seamlessly convert our visual field into a detailed awareness of all the elements in view and the relationships between them. Could I again master the spatial awareness needed to find a car's door handle without prompting, or to eat peas with a fork unassisted?

My analytical brain tried to create a flow chart of all the elements necessary to do a simple task like pouring a glass of water and found it impossibly complex. I realized that I am not a robot that can be programmed with set commands to accomplish a given task. My world is as dynamic and fluid as I am. The rapid data processing my world required would have to be learned in slow steps. The factual information could be stored in my brain, but the sensory data would have to accumulate in my body.

Getting from one place to another requires establishing where you are; establishing where you want to be; avoiding collision; conserving your psychic and emotional energy; and, finally, meeting a schedule unharmed. Imagine that you need a quart of milk. You go into the supermarket and scan for informational signs about the whereabouts of milk. Now you know where you are and where you want to be. You walk toward the milk aisle, continually scanning and repositioning yourself (distance, elapsed time) in relationship to the milk. You reach the shelf by the most direct route, having handily avoided collisions with people and produce. You reach out your hand, grab a quart of milk, and put it in your cart. Whole milk or low-fat? Your eyes and brain work together effortlessly, and you arrive home in time to have that late-night bowl of cornflakes.

I, on the other hand, have to go to a store whose layout I have learned through long study, first by building the backdrop of its layout, then by putting in the inventory item by item, as if building the scenery for a play and putting the props in place. Even then I need plenty of time, and I'm still liable to end up with orange juice.

Whether sighted or blind, we need reference landmarks to locate ourselves in a given space. From any position, and from each change in position, the sighted person instantly adjusts to any altered relationships. Missing any step along the way increases your confusion, disorientation, and accuracy of navigation, whether you and the objects are stationary, or you move and the objects move, or one party stays still while the other moves. When you go to an unfamiliar location (a shopping mall, for example) and fail to make a mental note such as "I am parked at Mervyn's and my car is halfway down the lot, near the left-hand door, in line with the hot-dog vendor," you haven't enough spatial information to find the car. Without complete information, you can wander for long minutes while your brain struggles to retrieve some spatial clue. The more time elapses, the greater the panic and disorientation factor, and the fainter the memory traces become. Then you have to do what the blind person does: go back into Mervyn's and retrace your steps in the hope that some sensory clue will trigger a buried memory. As with me, missing any step along the way increases your confusion, disorientation, and accuracy of navigation.

Close your eyes and imagine yourself in a featureless space without any walls—say in the middle of a broad plain, but without cornfields or grass or blue skies. There is no *up* or *down*. You do not know if you are *above* or *below* the features of the landscape. There is no *against* or *ahead*, no *along* or *among* or *around* or *beneath* or *beside*, no *between* or *from* or *in front of* or *in* or *out*, no *off* or *through* or *toward* or *under*, no *within* or *nearby*. All of these prepositions are abstract or metaphysical definitions, meaningless to someone blind. You are forced to construct some method for relating yourself and objects to these prepositions, accurately and in a reasonable time frame, without too many collisions.

In my typical grandiose way, I estimated that with my powers of concentration and memory I would master the elements of spatial relationships by the time the course was over. In fact, it took me five years to be able to navigate independently.

Our assignment the first day of class was to take a piece of paper and divide it into thirty-six sections by drawing a grid on the paper. The next step was to insert a drawing of a chosen object into each of the thirty-six sections and paint each section using a different color scheme. I spent the whole class trying to learn to use a twelve-inch ruler to draw a straight line on the twenty-two-by-thirty-inch sheet of paper. I was hopeless at this, but having at last abandoned my defeatist posture, I suspected that the task could be accomplished if I divided it into many elements.

I was soon stumped by the problems of drawing a series of equidistant parallel lines, both vertical and horizontal, on a piece of paper without a reference point. When I realized that I would need to create an imaginary starting point, the task became a little easier.

At lunchtime, I went to the store with a classmate and purchased a yardstick. I asked her how long an inch was and received an imprecise answer. So I asked someone to put a piece of tape at the one-inch mark on the yardstick and another at the one-foot mark. After lunch I was finally ready to do the exercise, only to discover that the lesson had changed. All that math, spatial analysis, and energy wasted on a task that should have taken but a few minutes. I couldn't keep up.

I was daydreaming in class, picturing myself as Lara Croft in *Tomb Raider,* fantasizing that I could move around this strange environment with her ease. (I go to the movies all the time and make up my own visuals.) Doug was lecturing about the principles of art, while I doodled and practiced drawing straight lines with my new yardstick. To fulfill my Lara Croft fantasy, I would need a way to determine the size of one object relative to another, and to arrange these shapes in a painting.

The term *linear perspective,* an offshoot of the concept of spatial relationships, came up. Someone commented that linear perspective is like parallel highway lines that appear to get closer, or converge, as they recede into the distance. Shapes and forms also become smaller and appear to recede. I perked up. This concept could help me resolve the problem of creating depth in my flat universe. In the real world, lines converge at the horizon, which is always at eye level. In my virtual constructs, the horizon is where I put it, just as an artist places the horizon in a painting where he chooses. Merely imagining putting a horizon into my own mental maps was giving my flat universe dimension.

Perception and proportion are the rules of the road; but the rules shift and change in the world of spatial relationships. For example, the apparent width relative to the length of a table will vary depending on where you are standing in a room, even though the actual size and shape of the table is fixed. The advantage to blindness is that in my world the table never changes proportions. It is always three feet by five. *Aha!* All of a sudden I'd understood something important about reaching out for objects, walking around obstacles, passing through a door. The prospect that the core concepts of art (such as linear perspective, contour, surface shading, shadow and light gradients) might offer concrete explanations to help me make sense of where I am, on a canvas or in a room, was so appealing that I would have given up my three-pack-a-day M&M's habit to know it all.

I'd already figured out how to line up my brushes left to right, from the largest to the smallest. To count the number of sweeps of my cane from my stool to the sink or the desk. Now if I could learn to draw a straight line, a square, a rectangle, a circle, and a cube, perhaps I could use acrylic paint to draw a map of the room's layout. I theorized that after I had the map, I could mentally transpose this schematic to a three-dimensional mental mock-up that would indicate foreground and background, distance and depth. This brain-grinding challenge took me far longer than two weeks to master. But using the principles of art, I learned to draw primitive shapes in relationship to a horizon line, correcting and erasing over and over until my lines and shapes did not collide, on a sheet of paper or in space.

For someone like me, with prior visual experience, the ability to relearn spatial relationships falls somewhere between learning a new cognitive map and recalling previous mental knowledge. Unlike a child blind from birth, the previously sighted person retains some sense of physical balance and coordination (both learned through spatial orientation) and has less fear of falling because of the "remembered" qualities of distance and dimension. Still, problems arise in the difficulty of specific identification. Air currents and crowd noise direct you to the door, but you may struggle to verify that it is the door you want. This is why many blind people will exactly retrace their steps, never varying their route, rather than attempt a shortcut, even though they have walked the same route through the same building for years. Researchers know that two-thirds of those with adult-onset blindness can achieve a high level of perceptual and symbolic spatial awareness, while only one-tenth of congenitally blind children can do so.

The world of darkness is not appreciably different from the world of light with regard to my mental representation of space. Identifying objects and their relationships within a space requires utilization of all the senses for rapid processing. The basic difference between the blind and the sighted is that they utilize different methods to process the same information about spatial relationships. When it comes to spatial relationships, sight is neither necessary nor sufficient, though it is certainly more efficient. When I go caving with Al, our perceptions and analyses of events are matched. Without ambient light, I have the ability to navigate a dark and confined space faster than Al can and with greater confidence. Al and I become equal. Our recollections and notes on a caving experience are the same. Of course, without the advantage of processing information in the "blink of an eye," it takes me far more time to make a decision and execute a move. When you lose your sight, everything takes longer. Your whole sense of time alters profoundly, and you are forced to scale down your expectations and your workload. You adjust your goals for what you can accomplish in a given time period, and what you can expend the energy to accomplish.

The passage of time also takes its toll on memory, no matter how good that memory is. For all my prodigious memory skills, for all my diligent efforts to keep my visual memory stimulated, to periodically review and refresh the filing cabinet of memory, the world inevitably fades. Without vision, you are forced to live in the small sector of the world that is within your reach, along with what you can keep alive in your brain. Try as you might, once-distinctive objects dissolve over time into amorphous shapes, losing their individuality and personal significance. Except for the ones you can touch, an ashtray, a frying pan, a lamp, a knickknack become concepts with generic shapes and functions. You can no longer remember the pink ashtray with the palm trees that says "Memento of Miami Beach." Landscapes flatten into schematic drawings; trees become more an intellectual concept than a reality. The notion of a layout or a map becomes fuzzy. Space is distorted by noise, which can make a twenty-by-forty room seem like a tiny cubicle. Silence can make a room seem cavernous.

Without vision it is easy to lose track of where one is in space, and even which way you are facing. A quick story can illustrate how the world fades without constant reinforcement. A few years after my stay in Ruston, Al put me on a plane to Dallas to visit a friend in my old neighborhood. Well aware of my ability to navigate on my own, she met me at the baggage claim. We decided to take the trolley to a restaurant. I hadn't been on a trolley since my vision loss, so she had to play leader.

I could get to the trolley unaided, but I had no concrete concept of the height from the road to the trolley steps. All details
regarding the trolley's number, name, locale, and platform, and
the placement of its seats, had evaporated from my memory,
and my friend was not able to fill in the missing information in
terms that I could use. There were curb cuts for wheelchairs
and auditory stop signals, my friend reported; there was a bell
pull to signal a stop. I realized that I was mobile but not oriented. Although I was quite proficient at using my cane to
avoid danger, orientation and spatial understanding of a new
environment would always require help and information from
others. I had forever lost the ability to apprehend the "whole-
ness" of my environment. I would have to be content with
what I could actually touch, smell, hear, and taste.

One day Doug was talking about the corners of a painting.
Even the corners have importance, he insisted. If they don't
draw the viewer's interest, by virtue of either their color or
their design, the painting loses some of its compositional force.
Few in the class understood the concept that in composition
there are three elements to consider: the frame (the edge of the
paper), the positive space (where the image is), and the negative space (where the image isn't). For a composition to work it
must strike a balance between positive and negative space. A
half hour passed, and the class wasn't getting it. I think sighted
people don't realize that edges and frames are as important as
background and foreground because they can always see
boundaries and don't need to think about them. Finally Doug
turned to me and said, "Explain this."

I used the analogy that I am the positive space, everything
outside me is the negative space, and the frame is the arbitrary

cutoff point that I determine for my mental construct of any given area or environment. The world is made up of shapes, positive forms with solid mass and obvious color. The space surrounding the forms merely indicates the negative, or the *absence,* of phenomena. The visual person automatically picks out the objects from the background. For someone with sight, negative shapes are not tangible forms, while to me the spaces between objects have substance and form equal to the positive spaces.

The concept of negative space is useful in both art and everyday life. In art, the concept of positive and negative space helps set the borders of a composition and define the objects within those borders. In a painting you give equal weight, or attention, to the negative and the positive. When painting the negative or background areas, you are by default shoving the positive to the foreground. By inducing the eye to see the negative you are creating a stronger compositional force.

In everyday life, an understanding of negative and positive space informs our body language and social interactions. Knowing others' physical and emotional boundaries is essential. Each of us has a physical comfort zone, an optimal distance between ourselves and those around us. Permission to encroach on that negative space is granted with a glance or a smile. Because I cannot read body language or react to facial clues, I think of people's positions in terms of positive and negative space. It helps me to picture myself in any social situation as we would appear on a canvas. I rely on intellectual knowledge of these imaginary boundaries, and use it to guide me in my social interactions. Attending to intonations and verbal cues, I attempt to position myself at the edge of your negative space. Misjudging distance and spatial relationships might bring me too close, and make you feel that I had invaded your space; too far and I would seem aloof. Understanding the concept of negative and positive space facilitates my own body language and prevents me from committing a social faux pas.

A grasp of positive and negative space helps me get around. To navigate safely, I must give equal attention to objects and the spaces in between them. The shared edges where the positive and negative meet are my compositional reality. There is always a frame, or edge, to my navigational field, beyond which my knowledge ends. I place objects on the scene, within the frame, just as I have learned to do on canvas, right to the edges. A white ball (positive) on a black background (negative space) on a rectangular piece of paper (frame) *equals* a white car (positive) on blacktop (negative) in a parking lot (frame). As on paper, so in a shopping mall. Eureka!

Sometime during the second week of class, I made the amazing discovery that spatial information can be accessed from a distance, not just from an arm's reach away or by going to a wall and reorienting myself from there. This ability to "scan" the environment is parallel to a toddler's letting go of the table when learning to walk.

The following incident may seem minor, but it opened a door I thought was forever closed. I was at a sink while someone else cleaned my brushes (yes, everyone was chipping in with the blind project) when I realized that I had a way to clean my own brushes. Why couldn't I just put the brushes into the brush cleaner, without putting my hands in the cleaner, and then wash them under the water? I could hear the water running in the metal sink, making a slow *plop plop plop* sound, and I thought, *This is right in front of me.* Then I noticed that the noises of the radio were in the *next* room and to the *left* of me and the sounds were muffled because they were *behind* a wall. The cacophonous din was sorting itself out into useful information that would transform my life. With my newfound auditory reach I could shower, could wash my hands in the restroom, could relax at the sound of approaching footsteps.

Then I noticed that my friend Mae was wearing a distinctive perfume, and that she shuffled when she walked. She had just entered the room and was walking *toward* me. Without thinking, I turned toward the sound and said, "Are we ready to go yet, Mae?" The woman washing my brushes was astounded. "How did you know that?" I asked her to verify my sense that I was eight feet from the paint-storage table, and sure enough I was. With each new expansion of my sensory reach, my stress level fell.

Everything seemed to be coming together at once, as though the hours of painting spatial relationships each day was seeping into my bones, opening up new perceptual channels. Air currents and noises were no longer just a muddled roar. They offered clues to my environment, and if I paid attention, I would just *know*. Other students remarked that I had begun to rotate my body toward the person speaking and was looking up at their face (I say "up" because I'm barely five feet tall). It felt as if my mind was waking from a deep torpor and my body was relearning to position itself in the world.

I'd been a sensory sleepwalker, turned in on myself, ignorant of environmental clues and paralyzed into believing that because the visual system rules the brain, there was no way to survive in a new environment without constant dependence on others. On that first day of class in June, I'd been pinned to my stool in a full-blown panic attack. Until now, though many helpful people were taking me by the hand and leading me to where I needed to be and putting a brush in my hand, I'd still been mentally stuck on that stool. Suddenly, I was free to roam.

The passing days brought a growing awareness not only that I was learning powerful new strategies for connecting to my surroundings but that I had an aptitude for art. *Jars* was beginner's luck, pure anger-fueled instinct. It was not a replicable experience. But now I was learning specific new techniques that seemed to translate directly from the canvas to the route back to the dorm. There would be a steep learning curve before I produced something recognizable. But the bottom line was that I loved this class, I loved to paint, and what I loved most was that painting was awakening glimmers of color and form in my gray inner world. I was beginning to understand that the distance between the water bottle on my desk and the statue "out there" paralleled the distance between my dorm room and the bathroom, which in turn paralleled the distance between two objects that I placed at will in my paintings. I was establishing for myself the relationship between navigating in the dark and mastering spatial relationships on the finite plane of a sheet of paper. I was coming up with answers for those who asked, "How do you do it?" The world was coming back to me.

CHAPTER SIX

PAINTING IN THE DARK

One must from time to time attempt things
that are beyond one's capacity.

—AUGUSTE RENOIR

RETURNING FROM RUSTON after the second session was a shock. I was home, alone. There was no art class. There was no one to take me for a walk. I was fired up to live in the world again, to be an artist, to reenter life. But I discovered that I had no life, since before Ruston I had lived in my bedroom in the dark. What I had now was merely existence.

I was furious that I had lost my freedom. In Ruston I could wander about on campus, feeling that I was engaging with the world. At home, there was only Al to talk to, day in and day out. I had no intimate friends nearby. Actually, I had no intimate friends anywhere. The woman who is now my closest friend was trying her best to penetrate my willful isolation, but she almost gave up. I first met Claudia shortly before I began to lose my vision, when she gave me my weekly manicure. What began as idle chitchat while I got my nails done turned, over the course of a year, to more intimate conversation—rare for me. We'd begun going to yard sales and making late-night forays to Wal-Mart.

When I began to lose my vision, I was alone, trapped, in precarious health. I was pushing all gestures of help or concern aside, pretending I could see and didn't need them. I couldn't accept myself, or my situation, but Claudia did. She refused to be bullied by my anger and rejection. Slowly I realized that I could trust her to keep my secrets, to listen and not judge me. Every time I performed some small task, like brushing my teeth or going outside to get the mail, she would point out how much better I felt. Claudia's matter-of-fact acceptance of me and my predicament challenged my picture of myself as isolated and rejected. I did my best to keep her at arm's length.

I had time, too much time, on my hands. For so many years I had dedicated myself to work obligations and made sure to fill up my days with household chores, shopping, movies, and social events. Now I was forced to sit back and wait—for transportation, for stimulation, for company, for food. I tried to explain how stifled I felt after my stay in Ruston, but no one could really understand. Yes, I could now find my socks and walk safely to the mailbox. I could perform the activities of daily living with little effort. But I found that eating, sleeping, and dressing were not enough. I desired—I still desire—a life of adventure and excitement, of change and challenge, one that would test my mettle as a human being. I kept thinking there had to be more than just *this*, that life could not possibly be reduced to eating, sleeping, and waiting. I was still waking up each morning shocked that I couldn't see. *Yikes, I'm blind.* I burrowed in my bedroom and stopped talking to everyone, Claudia included.

The problem was that by now I really couldn't see a thing. The grueling hours of classes, the stress of switching from one subject to another, from one exercise to another, had taken their toll. As my eyesight continued to fade, other complications of my vasculitis escalated. My asthma attacks multiplied. Allergic reactions to new foods arose. Problems with my blood pressure and kidneys slowed me down. My flagging energy was a serious impediment to my desire to take the world by storm.

I desperately needed a new life. What would that entail? I made an ambitious wish list of things to do. I would enroll in art school, get a job. I signed up for a painting class and a ceramics workshop. I was revved up to take piano lessons, master Braille, learn to sculpt, and practice yoga. I was energized psychically, if not physically. I applied for thirty jobs. Accounting, financial planning, pension-fund administration, insurance oversight, medical review. Often I would make the final cut only to be told that the company in question was not in a position to meet the ADA requirements.

My attempt to take art classes was a failure. In my first painting class the instructors insisted that I provide photographs or other visual references so that they would know what it was I was trying to paint. I signed up for painting seminars sponsored by our local watercolor group. Al would pack up my supplies, drive me in to Austin, help me set up the paints, and orient me to the bathroom. After class, someone would bring me home. In spite of my prickly defensiveness, I enjoyed the opportunity to socialize with other artists.

I tentatively made my first new friend. Bob was attending painting classes as part of his transition toward retirement. His wife, Marilyn, had no interest in art, so we would talk for hours about clay, about famous artists, and about self-expression. Eventually he discovered that art was not as exciting as golf, so he took me out on the course and taught me to use a wedge and an iron. Marilyn taught me to bake and play mah-jongg. Their concern and affection made hairline cracks in my brittle shell.

Then I decided to take a watercolor seminar taught by the well-known artist and author Jan Kunz. My fellow art-club members told me I would never be a competent painter until I learned her method for painting flowers. Another fiasco. She gave everyone a photocopy of one of her paintings to transfer onto their sheet of watercolor paper. The object was to learn to paint a glass vase filled with flowers by copying her drawing, colors, and technique. The class dutifully transferred the drawing onto their paper, and proceeded to complete their paintings with the colors suggested in her book. A concrete approach, perhaps, but impossible for me.

On the way home, one of the women said to me, "Isn't this stimulating? Now you know why we think you needed to take this class." They were clueless, and so was I. I may not have been able to handle the assignment, but what exactly were they learning by this rote method? I felt I had wasted my money. But the group prodded me on. "Lisa, you need to be more open to new experiences. You will just *love* the next seminar." The new seminar, however, turned out to be more "observe the photo, observe me" instruction. I guess this is how people learn to paint, but I couldn't see the nose on my own face, let alone a photograph. My frustration mounted.

Someone suggested that a basic pottery class might prove easier for someone blind. They were right. The first day the teacher explained that the course would cover hand building, throwing on the wheel, and drawing designs into the clay. It would probably take the full twelve weeks to learn to use the wheel, she declared, but the design work and hand building would be easier. I sat at the wheel and threw my first pot and it was centered, balanced, and correct. I was bored.

I decided to enroll at the local university. Maybe they had a better way for me to learn. The university had never had a blind art student, but they were receptive. My admission application required a portfolio. Of course I did not have a portfolio. No problem, I assured them, I can draw and paint. I was asked to draw a cylinder, cube, and sphere and shade them properly. To my surprise, I could not do any of these things. Ruston had led me to believe that mastery of the principles of art could lead me out of my dark cocoon. But apparently, I still couldn't produce a recognizable object. Again I went into a tailspin, convinced that I would never gain access to the mysteries of art. I had failed once more to join the world of the sighted. My attempt to create a new life was a bust.

———————

I was right, as usual. There was no help for me. I would have to find my own way, alone. Fed up with my attempts to make it in the world, I retreated to my room again, determined that I wouldn't come out until I could reenter the world on my own terms. I would teach myself to paint. I would conquer the dark void. *I'll show them.* Having proven unequal to my goal of being the best blind person ever, I was now determined to at least be the best painter. I have to laugh when I look back on this smug pronouncement. My obsessive nature, I can see now, was both my motivator and my downfall.

And so it began. Object by object, I began to rebuild my world. I'd spend hours, working through sheet after sheet of paper, drawing circles, squares, triangles. All sizes, each one better, more perfect than the one before. Hundreds of circles, thousands of triangles. I used tubes of T-shirt paint, which left raised lines I could trace with my fingers. Each day I got a little better, worked a little longer, surrounded by piles of crumpled paper.

Al was thrilled to see me engaged, impressed with what I was doing. He moved his cars, motorcycle gear, and collectibles over to one side of the garage, piling up boxes to the ceiling. Another windowless workspace for me, but it was mine, and the open door let in fresh air.

Every day was still a struggle, spent looking for a dropped brush, differentiating the shampoo from the conditioner, conserving my fluctuating energies, factoring a new chair into my carefully plotted navigational scheme. Now I could find my way to the kitchen, pour a glass of water. But I couldn't seem to get the hang of the microwave. I started drawing cubes, three-dimensional boxes, like my microwave. Day after day. Week after week. It seems simplistic, but it was a revelation. By the time I could draw a competent cube, I could also place a bowl in the microwave without spilling its contents. Something about creating the microwave shape freehand, on a sheet of paper, made what baffled me in the kitchen real, graspable.

Next I drew an object in that cube, to see what would fit inside. I drew bigger cubes and filled them with multiple objects, in complex arrangements. Rows of shapes, arranged from left to right, front to back. This gave me the courage to tackle my closet again. Heaven knows we'd tried to find a way for me to pick out my own clothes. But the "Where is my purple T-shirt?" issue persisted. We'd carefully sewn Braille labels into every item of clothing. It hadn't worked, since I could barely read Braille. The cube gave me a system I could understand, a space I could arrange. Now my gear could be managed, organized into a coherent system byte by byte.

Some of my experiments in spatial organization were successful, and others failed. But the whole process of finding alternative techniques to order space amazed me. The Greeks believed that direct vision was the first and final source of wisdom. My wisdom would have to come from other sources, namely logic and the rational mind; but how to retrain myself? All I knew was that I still had my intellect, and what Plato referred to as "a knowledge into the soul which was not there before, like sight into a blind eye." All I needed to do was to develop the ability to take a colorless, formless, and intangible essence and turn it into reality.

When I first began to lose my vision, I assumed that my other senses would rise to the occasion, helping me to adjust and change. I bought into the accepted wisdom that when you lose one sense, the others become heightened and take over. This is not quite what happens. Other people who lose their sight may have a different experience, but my hearing did not become more acute just because I was now blind. It's just that I paid more attention, and learned to extract more data from sounds. Even so, the information is limited. A dog barking or a baby crying is an indicator of location, but not of the sex of the child or the color of the dog.

Not all the senses are useful in establishing shapes or negotiating three-dimensional space. Smell and taste add to the richness of life, but they do not help me determine the size, distance, or relative position of the shower faucet. Smell and taste cannot help me draw a straight line on a sheet of paper. The sense of touch lacks the referencing schemes available through sight. When I touch a sheet of paper, I can distinguish texture, weight, and rag content, but not the paper's color or the writing on it.

My experience is that our senses are more interdependent than we realize. The brain depends on input from all its sources working together to tell it what's going on. When I began to lose my sight, my other senses also felt out of whack. I didn't seem to hear as well as before, and I had the sense of being off balance. Food tasted different when I couldn't see it. It seemed that my other senses were used to working in tandem with my eyes, and I felt discombobulated. I literally felt as if I couldn't think straight. As my hearing has diminished in recent years, I again have the sensation of my other senses atrophying. I have to rehabituate myself to this new sensory loss, and learn to compensate in some other way.

Through hearing, touch, and smell, I create a sensory bridge between the world and my body and soul. As I got my bearings, I began to extract more information from all incoming sensory data. I registered the air pressure of a cloudy day, the density and ozone smell of approaching rain, the slightest shift in the wind. The sound of falling rain on dissimilar surfaces delineated the surrounding landscape—the flower beds, the driveway, the porch overhang. I began to pick up the energetic presence of objects and people in my space.

I found myself "looking" for an object before I reached for it. I touched objects more often, trying to scan their surfaces with my fingers, tracing their borders and exploring their texture as a means to understand them and my lost world. To ensure that I understood an object's essence, I tried to feel it in a variety of settings (as you would view a statue from all sides). Just as when you look at a color steadily it begins to fade from consciousness, so too an object held motionless in the palm of my hand will vanish. I've learned that movement—of my hands or of my whole body—is critical. Without my own movement to reinforce an object's three-dimensional reality, I cannot get a sense of the whole.

I was learning as a child learns, by handling objects, then recreating the same shapes on paper and in clay. At some point the proverbial light bulb switched on, and an instinctual understanding of shapes kicked in. Increasingly often, the proposition "I see an object; I see the world around me" took on meaning. I became a master of inductive reasoning, with the ability to infer a larger environment or a whole set of circumstances from a minimum of clues. I know, for example, that the fuzzy white patch I can decipher when I enter my bedroom is my pillow. If there are no shapes as I walk along the sidewalk, I conclude that there is no barrier I might trip over. I know that the noisy, dark moving patches in the road indicate cars and buses. A wispy halo at eye level means someone is approaching me. If I know the context—office, front porch, dining room—then all I need is the distinguishing characteristic, the minimal form for me to make sense of the larger environment. In one setting, the large dark object is certainly a chair; in another, a doorway or a desk. Even in my world of shadow vision, the pattern stimulates a response.

Of course, this system works only with really large objects. It does not help me distinguish between a winter melon and a watermelon of the same size, a pen with blue ink versus one with black, shoes of different colors but the same material, and so on. Such general impressions can get you in trouble, as I learned when I got separated from Al recently at Foley's department store. Or, to tell Al's version of the story, when I wandered away in my usual determination to assert my independence. I retraced my steps, trying to relocate him. Immensely pleased that I had navigated back to him without requiring help, I put my arms around his waist and gave him a big kiss. Only to discover that the large object wearing jeans and a T-shirt was not Al at all.

Using my remaining senses to perceive and then to mentally integrate my perceptions, I was developing a powerful and functional alternative to visual perception. There is a way in which I "project" sensory input and intellectually acquired information onto an internal screen, so that it coalesces into imagery. The Chinese believe that the master paints not the created thing but the forces that created it. It seemed to me that I was beginning to paint energy as much as form. I can only compare it to a kind of full-body vision.

Having mastered the basic shapes and concepts of design, I attempted to combine the shapes in paintings, using my new-found understanding of spatial order. I carefully planned the compositions and color balance, only to be told yet again that the result was a kind of monochromatic mud. I lived in the studio, day after day, night after night, barely emerging for food and sleep. All the while I chanted my mantra under my breath: *I hate you all; I'll show you.* My golfing friend Bob became bored with retirement and took a job that transferred him to Tennessee. Claudia was overwhelmed taking care of her family, which was just as well, because I was still trying to keep her from getting too close. So I was again alone.

But who needed friends? I was on a quest to be the perfect painter. In my world, day and night were indistinguishable. I loved my world. Here I was in control, here no one could remind me of my shortcomings. And so I hid out in art, rejecting everything beyond my door, secretly nurturing a hope for some revelation of where my life was going.

While I waited, I forged ahead. In my wide-ranging travels, I'd paid no attention to the treasure troves of art in the museums and galleries, cathedrals and castles along the way. I'd missed the Prado and the Louvre, Notre Dame and Giverny, preferring to spend my time shopping or people watching on the Champs-Elysée. Now I was hungry to know everything about art. I badgered Al to read me every art book we could find. Hour after hour, he read to me about the lives of artists and schools of art. We plowed through dense analyses of painting and color theory, treatises on composition, esoteric theories of design, and reams of indecipherable art criticism. I formed my own ideas about technique and style, and adopted my own favorites in Degas, Delacroix, Homer, Sargent, and Reynolds. In recent years, Al has been my seeing-eye guide as we made the rounds of the art citadels I can no longer see. I deeply regret that I had no interest in art before I lost my sight. My internal picture of Degas's dancers is constructed entirely from secondhand information that I have no way of verifying.

I trained myself to differentiate watercolor pigments by their texture. I would practice for hours, rubbing a small drop of paint between my fingers, then having Al quiz me as to the color I was touching. Blue or red or yellow? After about three months, I could identify the primary colors. I experimented with different types of palette layouts, those that mirror the color wheel and others that lay out the colors in squares and rectangles. My goal was to be able to mix a primary color into a complement (orange, purple, green). I bored everyone in earshot with my ideas on color theory. People began to ask me how to mix the perfect orange, gray, green, or violet, and I could tell them precisely. Al read me more books on color, watercolors in particular. I spent hours creating examples in my head on the technical properties of color. Then I decided I had to know everything about watercolor papers: their rag content, absorbency, and weaves, their technical properties, and the optimum applications for each type and manufacturer. From there it was watercolor brushes, mediums, pencils—any tool involved in painting watercolors. If I was going to be the best painter, given my minor handicap, I certainly had to learn every aspect of technique and materials.

But Al was worried. I was practically incommunicado in my dark lair, and the signs of my obsession were getting worse. I paid no attention to day or night, to hygiene, food, or sleep. Al did everything in his power to get me back to the local art guild, where I could paint with other people and have a social life. For many months, I resisted his efforts, confident that insight would emerge if I studied hard enough.

Once he dragged me out of hiding, though, I enjoyed the break and felt welcome. The guild held an open show where all the members of the group could enter one or two paintings for a small fee. I entered a still life of onions that I'd labored over for three class sessions. The judge thought they were balloons.

No, not again. After so many months in my studio bunker perfecting my knowledge and mastery of art, I was devastated to realize that I still couldn't paint a recognizable object. In a snit, I cut the painting up and turned it into paper weavings. Then I had to deal with my classmates calling to commiserate and to offer insight into my feelings. My feelings? *Oh puhleeze.* Some suggested that the rejection was not good for me. It was a wake-up call to the folly of my trying to be an artist, a sign that I should not be entering competitions. Others felt that I was using my blindness as a lever to gain entrance into the shows, and this episode was an example of my desire to get attention. Someone I had never spoken to in class called to say that I'd had no right to enter, since I would never be able to paint as well as someone sighted. "Why do you have to paint?" she wanted to know. "Why don't you enter art competitions for the visually impaired?" I was incensed.

And I was embarrassed. The irony is that I now realize that my goals differed from those of a sighted painter. I was operating under a different set of rules. I was trying to learn to paint and draw as a method for re-creating a world now lost. My agenda was not to win exhibitions but to have an impartial observer validate what I was seeing in my head. Because I was still so inept at portraying the visual world, it was not so surprising that others would challenge my motivation for wanting to learn this obviously visual skill.

My foray into the world of painting competition brought up other issues. People would ask why I used a cane. Some were annoyed if I accidentally rapped them on their heels, snapping, "Can't you watch where you are going?" I discovered that people would say anything to me. No question was off-limits. Strangers would tell me that they expected me to have no body language, or enucleated eyes. People commented on perceived mistakes in my paintings that they attributed to my blindness. Not infrequently, people talked about me in the third person as though I were not in the room or I were mentally feeble. It was not uncommon for people to shout, as though they expected me to be hard of hearing as well, or to direct their questions to Al. Others would grab me by the arm to show me something, then get angry when I could not see it. They would pull out their vacation photographs and expect me to comment on them.

When I groused about this insensitive treatment to Claudia, she told me that Helen Keller was considered such a freak that she and her teacher, Annie Sullivan, actually did a vaudeville act to make money and survive. Claudia's point was that I would have to learn to live with people's responses to my abilities and not be so oversensitive. About a year later Claudia and I were in downtown Georgetown when a woman came up to say that it was a pity I couldn't dress myself properly. I was wearing my usual painting ensemble of baggy cotton pants, Grateful Dead T-shirt, funky socks, and pink bedroom slippers with rabbits on the toes. I was about to make a nasty retort when Claudia began describing the woman's outfit to me. What was she wearing? A beaded red sweater, leopard-pattern tights, and a violet fake-fur purse to offset her bright copper-colored hair.

Claudia says this incident marked the day I began to have a sense of humor in response to others' curiosity.

I kept thinking that if I were not blind these issues would never have come up. *Well, of course not, because I would have painted a recognizable onion.* I could not understand why my onion painting was not accepted purely as a poor painting, a bad day at the easel. Nothing more and nothing less, not a judgment about my desire to paint as a blind person. Why were they holding me to different standards? Of course they weren't. They were simply judging me as they would a sighted person. It is testimony to my defensiveness that I couldn't understand that most sighted people would have been able paint a recognizable onion.

Back to the studio I went, in a fury. My rallying cry—*I hate you all. I'll show you!*—spurred me on. More determined than ever to learn to paint and regain a sense of normalcy, I did twenty more onion paintings. I didn't quit until everyone immediately recognized the subject matter as onions. Only much later could I admit that these paintings, while readable, finally, were in no way works of art.

One day someone mentioned a large juried show coming up in San Antonio. The judges were going to accept one hundred paintings from among the regional guilds in the state. Most of the two hundred members of my local group entered, as it was a preliminary step to membership in the American Watercolor Society. Recovering from the onion debacle, I submitted three paintings. Concerned friends warned me that the pieces were likely to be rejected; they did not want to see me upset again. Others were fed up with my refusal to accept that I was blind. Well, I was accepting that I was blind, more each day. What I was not accepting was people's inability to get past the fact that I was blind. In the art guild classes I had redoubled my efforts to produce something recognizable and had painted three watercolors. All three of my pieces, *Tropical Tiger, California Bantams,* and *Doug's Birthday,* were accepted into the show. The judges probably assumed that the paintings were the work of three different artists, as each theme was different.

The minute the acceptance list was posted I began receiving calls. Al was glad that I was beginning to socialize again and make friends. But my reaction was more mixed—since the response was mixed. Not everyone was thrilled that I'd gotten in, in particular those who'd been rejected. The negativity ran from "If I hadn't seen you paint the piece, I would never have believed it" to "You did not deserve to make it into the show" and "What are you trying to prove?" As the week progressed, I stopped attempting to defend myself and just quit answering the phone. I was not sure of myself as a person, let alone an artist, and I was still insecure about my position in the world.

I was doing something that seemed "impossible" for a blind person to do, and I was beginning to do it better than some of my sighted peers. When I won second prize, no one called to congratulate me. This incident was a milestone in my love/hate relationship with art. Am I really an artist? Am I wrong to persist in learning to paint? Will I lose friends if I am successful? Are people giving me extra consideration because I'm blind? Are my paintings any good? It's an agony I struggled with for years. In truth, it hasn't entirely gone away.

Whatever my personal torment, my winning a ribbon reinforced Al's conviction that I was meant to paint. He believed that I had a gift that needed to be shared. Always my biggest fan, Al wanted to encourage me to keep painting, which meant to keep showing my work. Besides, he'd just been given his official disability retirement, and he didn't want to spend his days mowing the lawn. Hearing that there were street fairs and art festivals all over the country, he began to research the logistics of entry requirements and exhibit facilities. As a test, he sent slides of my work to the Main Street Fort Worth Arts Festival, one of the largest outdoor art fairs in the country. I was accepted. Al rustled up the gear we'd need for the show. He pulled together a borrowed tent and display panels, picture folios, rigging, tables and a couple of deck chairs, a cash box, and a credit card machine. He even improvised weights, from sections of PVC pipe filled with sand, to keep our tent in place. We framed my work with yard-sale finds and frames from a discount shop. And off we went to Fort Worth for the four-day event.

The intense prep work gave us an idea of the amount of labor and logistics involved in these street fairs. My old pension-fund ally, Martha, who now lived in Dallas, came and helped us set up. Exhausted already, we'd barely sat down when one of the judges came by and made a beeline for *California Bantams,* a painting she'd noted during the entry judging. "Thank God it's still here," she panted. "How much is it?"

For all our preparation, we hadn't actually considered prices, though theoretically selling art was the point of all this work. We had no idea how much to charge. *California Bantams* was a favorite of Al's; it had been hanging on our living room wall. He wasn't about to give it away, so he named an exorbitant price. "It's expensive," he warned. "A thousand dollars. Plus tax."

"That's why they invented plastic." She whipped out her credit card and paid our outrageous price without blinking. We were stunned.

Opening day was balmy, for a couple of hours. Then, typical of Fort Worth in March, the temperature plummeted to thirty degrees. The drunks came out and the wind came up that night. The next day, Friday, the show opened and closed eleven times in response to tornado warnings. Each time we had to take down the paintings; store the chairs, tables, and equipment; and batten down our small tent, which was located under a larger circus tent.

Between sieges, we hung out in a local bar with the other exhibitors, drinking beer or coffee, sipping split-pea soup, and singing Irish songs. It was a carnival atmosphere, and we were the carnies. All we lacked were elephants and a trapeze act. It was great fun, more fun than I could remember having had for a long, long while. We were immediately welcomed into the family of artists who traveled the festival circuit. Everyone we ran into freely shared their stories and their advice. I felt the stirrings of a new life.

On Saturday morning a tornado raged through the fair, taking with it the large circus tent that sheltered us. When we returned after the all-clear siren, everything was covered with broken glass and pottery shards. A ticker-tape parade of paper drifted in the air. The glass artist to our left had lost everything, and about half the work of the potter on our right was in smithereens. We'd fared far better. A few of the mats were damp, and a couple of watercolor originals were smeared. Still, we spent the remainder of the day cleaning up. Finally the sun peeked out, but the crowds didn't return.

Three days of high winds and cold were getting to me. I was ready to go home, but Al was too tired to pack up and insisted that we stay for the final day. We got into one of our rare rows, in front of Martha. I was being melodramatic, ranting about how no one was going to take me, or my work, seriously. I'd sold a painting, and that was enough. "The weather is a sign that I'm not supposed to do this," I pronounced.

"You pack up the tent then," Al said. "I'm going back to the hotel." That stopped me. And so it was that we returned to our hotel, a seedy affair barely more than a flophouse, and sank into an exhausted sleep.

On a sunny, humid, eighty-eight-degree Sunday morning, we returned to find that a street person had slept in our tent, leaving a note scrawled on a paper bag. "This is the most beautiful art I have ever seen. It is a joy to sleep in such pleasant surroundings. I have no way of paying for the painting I took, but I have left you something dear to me." He had "purchased" a small unframed watercolor in exchange for an empty Coke can with a plastic flower stuck in it. I was touched.

I was still tired, however, and whined about wanting to go home. I was badgering Al when a tide of people surged along the sidewalks and I began to sell my work. Over the next six hours, we made an additional thirteen thousand dollars. Perverse and cranky as always, I announced that I was exhausted, and it was all too much work and I would never do another show. Al got angrier and angrier, again insisting that I had a gift that needed to be shared with the world.

Just as Al finished packing up our first load of equipment and began to dolly it to the van, about eight long blocks away, our street person and his pals showed up. His ragtag cohort packed everything up in two hours flat. Al brought the van around, and they loaded us up. We bought them pizza and beer and gave them each an original eight-by-ten watercolor.

Al was jazzed. Today Fort Worth, tomorrow the world. "Get in there and paint, Lisa," he decreed. "We're going on the road."

CHAPTER SEVEN

ON THE ROAD

*Art is not what you see but what you make
others see.*
—EDGAR DEGAS

A L TACKLED OUR NEW LIFE PLAN with his usual zeal. He
took that fourteen grand and plowed it back into our new
business, buying a Chevrolet van and a twenty-eight-foot travel
trailer. He researched tents, panels, rigging, lights, labels, and
packing boxes. He arranged for Visa and MasterCard processing. He subscribed to *Sunshine Artist*, the magazine of the show
circuit, and pored over the festival calendars, state by state, to
find the most profitable shows in locations where we wanted to
travel. He sent off the application forms and slides of my work
to a dozen shows. I was accepted to nine of them. For once I
wasn't defensive when I was rejected. I figured I was still learning, so the occasional rejection was to be expected.

The term *blind jurying* appealed to me. In fact, Al called
our new venture Blind Ambition Studios. After my initial panic
about life on the road, I realized I was ready for this change. I
was primed to leave suburbia, ready to give up my self-imposed
isolation. I wanted to challenge my new skills, in art and in life.
I'd had such a good time with the other artists at the Fort
Worth fair. Life on the road held out the promise of a lively
escape from my doldrums. If Al was so keen to join the art circuit and show my work at street fairs, I figured, what the heck.

We'd certainly made good money in Fort Worth. Maybe Al wasn't so crazy to think that it was a good way to supplement his pension. I happily painted new pictures, mostly abstracts and simple still lifes.

And so it was that for the next three years we traveled the country, doing the art-festival circuit, in places from Chicago to Albuquerque to Palm Springs, where slides of my work had been selected by juries who had no idea I was blind. This was a wonderful time for us. We were traveling, which we both loved. We were making money, which we both loved. Our adversarial relationship became conspiratorial. We had become a team, with shared goals. We were having fun, meeting people at the fairs, and striking up friendships with the regulars on the circuit, some of which developed into enduring ties. On our way to or from the fairs, we'd often spend a few days relaxing and sightseeing. New places and new people became a major source of nourishment for my vision-starved brain, and for my work.

Of course, not every fair made money for us. Not every fair was a good fit for my style of painting. Not every fair was a barrel of fun. Many shows were back to back, several hundred miles apart. We might drive twelve to fourteen hours in one day to reach the next show. Show setups and breakdowns constituted extreme physical labor. Parking was always a problem. We would usually have to dolly our gear for many blocks from the van to the fair site, and for some reason it always seemed to rain on setup or breakdown day. A typical show setup took four hours the night before the show. It would usually be close to midnight when we fell into bed. The next morning we'd be up at six A.M. for the drive to the fair. After several trips dollying the artwork to the booth, Al would spend another hour hanging and pricing the artwork. No matter how organized he was, he always scrambled to be ready on time for the nine A.M. show opening.

Then we'd sit and wait. We never knew who would come into the booth, what kind of questions people would have, what paintings would sell. But feast or famine, rain or shine, we'd be on duty until the show closed, around nine. Again Al would pack up the art, dolly it back to the safety of the van, and we'd head out to dinner with our exhibitor colleagues to talk about the day's events and have a few laughs.

We did a show called the People's Art Fair in Denver. This show, we quickly figured out, had little to do with art and a lot to do with lifestyle options. The predominant fare in the vendors' booths was jewelry for piercings, New Age crystals, homeopathic remedies, retro sixties leather goods, skateboards, and head-shop paraphernalia. The attendees ranged across the social spectrum. Retired couples in Bermuda shorts and halter tops and neo-hippies on skateboards or inline skates, wearing little more than thongs, mixed with young mothers with Walkman headsets, jogging with their infants in high-tech prams. Cell-phoning teenagers in all manner of braids, dreads, and shaven heads, slathered with suntan oil, mingled with office workers carrying briefcases and brown-bag lunches. It felt like a nineties version of the sixties. Al remarked that he'd certainly misread the flavor of this fair from the brochure, and he vowed to do better research into future shows.

Since it didn't look like we'd be selling anything, our best option was to sit back and enjoy the scene. Al began a running discourse on the crowd, describing the people, their costumes, demeanor, and appearance, while I eavesdropped on their conversations. Then I took a turn describing the scene, inferring the mannerisms, appearance, dress, and attitude of people in the passing crowd from their conversation. Al would verify or, more often, correct my fanciful observations, and we would go on to create a story around the crowd. This grand diversion helped us pass the two days in Denver, and many future idle intervals in our art-fair ramblings.

Today I use a similar storytelling technique whenever I begin a new painting. I found early on that I could not paint without auditory stimuli. I need constant interaction with people, music, weather, and environmental sounds. I listen to music CDs, talk radio, or audiobooks while I paint. A brief news item on the radio might provoke mental pictures of the place and people involved. These first impressions are then amplified, adjusted, changed, and simplified in my imagination. I redraw, redesign, and restructure the vignette in my head until the concept takes on a tangible form. I mull over the painting in terms of such characteristics as verve and power and emotional tone, envisioning the color palette. Somehow I keep adding to the imagery in my mind, basing it on what I remember. I assume that over time my memory distorts my perceptions, but it concerns me less and less. The painting is my personal telling of the story, and I expect that my idiosyncratic mode of interpreting experience infuses my canvases with a unique energy.

Only when I've got it all figured out do I stand at the easel and paint. The actual application of paint to canvas or paper is the final step in a process that simmers and boils in my head for months.

Knowing we were unlikely to recoup our investment at the People's Art Fair, we tried to find a campground near Denver. No such luck. So Al checked us into a downtown motel that met our tight budgetary requirements. It soon dawned on us that this hotel, across from the local shelter, catered to, shall we say, hourly guests. I think the penny dropped when I asked the motel owner for towels and he charged me a deposit. We were both exhausted after a day in the Denver sun and decided we could tough it out for the night. There we were in a king-size bed with a shiny gold lamé spread over a mattress that would vibrate for quarters, with a broken air conditioner in the ninety-degree heat, a slow trickle of hot water that quickly turned cold, and pay-for-porn TV. We turned to each other and laughed. So much for the romance of the bohemian life.

We were still giggling an hour later when the room next door changed guests and the new occupants played "(I Can't Get No) Satisfaction" at full volume for their full hour. Escaping to the dingy corridor in search of ice and sodas, we were propositioned for a threesome. Trying to ignore the flower-entwined "I Love Mom" tattoo across our suitor's chest, Al told the man that we'd take him up on the offer if we couldn't make it as street artists. I did not sell one painting in Denver, but the memory is still good for a chuckle.

When we'd decided to try the festival circuit, Al and I had had several conversations about whether admitting I was blind would be a benefit or a hindrance. So far, I had been selling consistently at fairs where the majority of the people did not realize I could not see. For me it was a perfect situation, anonymity and painting. In the early years of losing my sight, I'd been so upset by the negativity and misconceptions about blindness that I was reluctant to do anything now that would open me to these experiences again. Al thought that I was being irrational and defensive. He believed that disclosing my

blindness on the entry form might result in special consideration being given to my safety and well-being. Despite my reservations, Al for the first time wrote, "the artist is blind" on the
entry form for a major show in Indianapolis in 1997.

Well, Indianapolis answered the "don't ask, don't tell"
question. The show was held on the local minor-league baseball
diamond. There was only one obstacle on the entire lot, a large
tree with sprawling roots located on a slope behind a bent
chain-link fence at the back end of the field. Guess where I
ended up? The show officials had relegated us to a spot where
all the obstacles converged, against the chain-link fence, behind
the tree, next to the volunteers' station. Potential viewers had
to go through the local potters guild booth to get to mine.
There was no way I could maneuver safely, and no way to leave
the booth on my own. Al had to close the tent and accompany
me every time I wanted to go to the bathroom. He complained
to the officials about the safety hazards and pointed out several
vacant obstacle-free spots where we might relocate, but they
wouldn't budge. They went so far as to tell him not to apply
next year, as it was "too much trouble" to accommodate someone blind.

Al was livid. He took a vibrant all-red abstract painting of
mine called *Acapulco Fire* that was visible from over a hundred
feet away and hung it in front of the booth as a kind of protest.
As we sat there in an angry stew, people starting streaming into
the potters' booth—and on to ours. That big red painting was
the "star" that allowed people to find the "blind painter."

The potters were really annoyed. They complained to the
show officials, who asked Al to take down the red painting.
This was the only street show I ever sold out in one day. We'd
arrived at the show with forty-two originals (all but five were
abstracts) and about two hundred reproductions. At the end of

the day they were all gone, so Al began to take down the tent and stack the empty boxes and chairs. Now the show officials decreed that we had to stay another day or we would never get back into the show. Al just laughed as he continued to pack up the booth. We were signed up to do a show in Michigan the following week, but with nothing left to sell, we spent a lazy week at Sleeping Bear Dunes before heading home. *Lazy* is the operative word. We did nothing but sleep and make love. The ability to enjoy sex is one of the few things you don't lose when your vision goes, though it changes without visual input. Self-consciousness is gone; you forget about your wrinkles and just act on your desire. Sex is the one place where I can let my defenses down and explore my fantasies without fear that my dark demons will arise to devour me.

We'd usually come home between trips. Al would catch up on business, scouting the fairs that would take us to interesting places, sending in the entry forms, tending to details of shipping and customer service. With the profits from my paintings, he built me a new studio that exactly fit my needs. Now I had, all within easy reach, large flat storage drawers for watercolor paper and finished work; brush stands that wouldn't tip over; drawers where paints could be organized in trays by color; an accessible sink with lots of counter space; a combined radio, CD, and tape player; and three rolling easels so that I could work on multiple paintings at once. An orderly, accessible, easily maintained haven.

I'd paint during these layovers, producing new work to take on the road, expanding my understanding and technique along the way. Though I was still doing abstracts, perfecting my ability to work with the principles of design and to create an interesting composition, I became more confident at painting still-life compositions. I would set up objects on the tabletop in my studio, and through a laborious process that combined touch with imagination, paint a pair of scissors lying next to a pitcher of flowers or a bowl of fruit. As I gained confidence in the logistics of managing the space on a sheet of paper, I was discovering that art goes beyond the basic principles of line, color, and perspective. Now that I could work with basic shapes and composition, could show depth and perspective and contour, I found my attention turning to aesthetic nuances such as balance, movement, and integration.

Refinements in my knowledge and technique carried over into life itself, at which I was simultaneously becoming more proficient. I had more confidence in my mobility, a more assured grasp of my surroundings. I felt more at home in the world, and with people. I kept in touch with many of our new-found friends on the art circuit. It seemed that I was popular, valued for my good humor and good counsel. Was it possible that, at last, I belonged? It dawned on me that my painting was transforming me, from the inside out.

Friends were too. Whenever we came off the road, I couldn't wait to see Claudia. I'd tried hard to push her away, but she insisted on being part of my life. Yes, I had a life now. I could see that I was going to be okay and that there was nothing shameful about tripping over a doorstep or spilling tea on my blouse. Claudia reminded me recently that I began to stop feeling sorry for myself when I discovered that over one hundred million Americans live with a chronic disease, and half of them are forced to curtail their activities in some way. My friend Sylvia claims that my natural restlessness eventually overcame my fear of living. She knew I was on the mend when I started calling her to go shopping or to a movie. Claudia says I've changed "in all ways," that today I am like a child without fear. It is hard for me to think that life is difficult when I have such dear pals in my life.

In March 1998, we traveled to Fairhope, Alabama, for a huge annual art show that draws legions of top-level fine artists and crafters. Anticipating warm sunny weather, Al and I wore lightweight clothing to the show. One minute we were swilling Cokes and complaining about the heat. The sandal-clad Florida jeweler on one side of us and the photographer from Atlanta on the other were mopping their sweaty brows when suddenly a brisk wind came up and the sky clouded over. The next minute brought a deluge of freezing rain. Our dog, Wizard, was suddenly everyone's best friend, as they lured him with cheese and peanut butter to climb onto their laps and keep them warm.

A woman in a dripping trench coat and umbrella sailed into our tent to escape the storm and bought two paintings while she awaited a break in the weather. It turned out that she was touring the gardens and antebellum sites of the South with eight women friends from Atlanta. An hour later another of her group, also soaking wet, happened into the booth and purchased a painting. A third woman followed, then another and another, until every one of the eight had bought at least one painting. They told Al that no one could decide which of the paintings they liked best, so this way they would be able to rotate them between their houses.

By 1998, Al had refined his ability to choose only high-quality shows with interesting regional diversity and good sales potential. As my artistic skills strengthened, I was being accepted to about 80 percent of the shows I applied to. But the years of travel began to wear on us. Al was tired of the long driving stints, the constant setup and breakdown. He was losing patience with the endless details of running our on-the-road business. In June 1999 we decided, for our twenty-fifth wedding anniversary, to do our last street show. Off we went to Omaha, Nebraska, to hang out with Nick and Terri Lees, a fellow artist and his wife we had met in Fairhope two years earlier. Nick, the goodwill ambassador for the Omaha show, thought it would be a great farewell venue for us. At Nick's insistence, I was interviewed on a local radio call-in show. The switchboard was swamped with calls, so the scheduled fifteen-minute spot extended to an hour and half. Al thought it was great that I was beginning to attract regional press coverage.

But the more press I received, the worse I felt. All my long-standing insecurities resurfaced. The wave of attention reminded me yet again that I was different. People's reactions to learning I was blind ranged from skeptical to mystified, from hostile to indifferent to confused. I was more confused than anyone. I certainly didn't want pity, but I felt I should be congratulated for having overcome obstacles. The petulant child in me felt I should be praised just for doing this amazing thing that many sighted people can't do. On the other hand, I resented having my blindness pointed out to me; I wanted to be treated just like any sighted artist. I wanted to belong *and* I wanted people to ooh and aah over my special talents. I sought approval, but I didn't want to explain blindness or my compulsive need to paint. My ambivalence only added to my insecurity. At the center of my stubborn denial that my blindness set me apart lay an insoluble conundrum. I had no way of knowing if my paintings were, in fact, any good, an issue that my blindness rendered me uniquely unable to resolve. It was a double-edged sword that was bound to wound me.

In my attempt to repair and return to "normal," I failed to recognize that the stonewalling strategy of my youth was not serving me here. I viewed every stranger's question as an attack on my personal survival. I saw no benefit in admitting to others that my life had changed irrevocably. I needed people, as well as the healing and affirmation they could provide. But I alienated them with my every word and action.

I would leave our booth to venture out by myself, walking the shows in order to avoid talking to someone about my lack of sight. If I couldn't physically escape, I would just stop talking. I was uncomfortable answering questions that fed misconceptions about blindness, questions that reeked of ignorance and idle curiosity. I couldn't bear it that people thought of my blindness as a disability. I hated the *disabled* label. Wasn't I like everyone else? Being blind is like being blond, I'd insist. It just is.

After the Indianapolis experience, I was adamant about not wanting to admit I was blind. I felt that if people knew my status, my sales would drop, while thoughtless and unkind remarks would increase. I know, I know: the sellout show in Indianapolis should have disabused me of this notion, but it hadn't. That's how confused I was. My reasoning was that all too often when someone noticed my cane instead of purchasing a painting, they would exclaim, "What a gift from God!" and want to pray over me. "Congratulations," others would chirp. "Keep up the good work." Or they'd ask, "Who really painted this?" People would touch me unexpectedly, posing personal questions and prying into my life. As far as I could tell, being blind as a painter was a detriment. I felt as if I was being asked to justify my existence. I had no answers as to why I had decided to paint and how painting was changing my life. I was mystified that I was expected to be a role model. Succumbing to the demand to expose myself, divulging the gory details of how I'd learned to live with this terrible affliction, was not my style. I thought I had adjusted and was evolving into a whole and contented personality. Unfortunately, to many people I would always be, first and foremost, blind.

I could accept criticism that found fault with the color or the theme or the general style of my artwork. What I had problems accepting were comments like "It must be a hoax" or "She doesn't look blind." Worst was the "Let's test it" approach, which involved putting obstacles in my path, to see if I'd trip over them, or waving something in front of my eyes to see if I would respond. "Just between you and me," went another one that rankled, "exactly how blind are you?" When I would explain my particular level of vision loss, it would reinforce their doubts. "Oh, so you can see light—that explains it. You're not really blind." Or "Since you weren't born blind, you remember how to paint."

"Sure. Just try it for fifteen minutes and get back to me," I wanted to say. Al told me to cut the sarcasm, to smile away the cynicism, and simply answer the questions. He said if I thought of myself as an educational ambassador for the blind, eventually people's perceptions would change. He was right, of course, but it was a two-way street, and my negativity was blocking the way. Slowly but surely, as my capablities and comfort level rose, the chip on my shoulder shrunk, and my perceptions of people's motives softened. By 2001, I had established myself as someone who could articulate the issues of blindness. Now I regularly receive e-mails requesting information about art, blindness, and living with a chronic illness.

Scientists and graduate students from around the world began to seek out my perspective on the problems of vision and perception. They too want to know how I do what I do. But in their case it's not idle curiosity. My ability to articulate my experience helps them develop new adaptive modalities for the blind. Have I written anything about my techniques of navigation and spatial awareness, a Danish engineer asks. A Japanese graphic artist calls to find out if I have a book about color or design that might help a programmer improve a video game. An Australian software designer inquires about writing a lesson plan to teach art to the blind or visually impaired.

Doctoral candidates from dozens of universities—from Milan and Düsseldorf and Delhi to Princeton and Columbia and Stanford—contact me in the hope that my personal experience will validate their research. "I've heard all about you," they begin, "and I just want to check out this one thing for my thesis." They want concrete input from someone who can describe the experience of blindness. They know that I can articulate the means by which I compensate for one sensory path via another. They inquire about how my insight into spatial relationships can help them build a better computer-animation program or strengthen a robotic arm. They are hoping that I can explain the thought process that enables me to retain visual imagery in my brain. They wonder if the visual imagery in my mind stimulates the visual cortex in the same way that actual seeing does. They are looking for insight into the astronaut's orientation in space, the dyslexic's brain disorder.

Sometimes the questions concern the possible connection between my vasculitis and my asthma or migraines. They are seeking a link between my childhood illnesses and my current situation, to see how long my condition went undiagnosed and how it played out over time.

Go to www.berkeley.edu.projects and you'll find me written up under "constructing moving pictures eyes-free." At www.harvard.edu, I'm under "imagine you can no longer see"; at www.nadc.ucla.com it's "arts and disabilities." Recently the director of Harvard Medical School's Center for Visual Rehabilitation contacted me about purchasing my paintings. "We are great admirers of your work," he wrote, "and feel that displaying it here would . . . serve as a great motivation for patients and staff."

There are millions of blind and visually impaired people who stand to benefit from technological advances to which my insight and observations might contribute. It's been immensely gratifying for me to be of help in this research, and to have my intellectual rigor and years of study validated.

For all my conflict about how I was treated and whether I was a decent painter, I was making my way as an artist. Many people who bought my paintings realized I was blind, of course. However, I had been accepted at each show on my own merits. Those who bought my paintings seemed to like my colorful style. My enjoyment lies in giving others pleasure, sharing the experience of lively color, and stimulating their visual palate. I like having my own inner vision corroborated by the sighted person. Al reassures me that people buy my work because my paintings touch something inside them. I was relieved and grateful to have emerged from my dungeon of darkness and depression. Al and I were best friends. Life had dealt us some hard knocks, and had softened us up in the process. For all my prickly fragility, I was building a life that was in many ways better than the one I'd led before I'd lost my sight.

In preparation for coming off the road, I contacted several art publishing houses with the idea of marketing my art on greeting cards, posters, and limited edition prints. Several publishers responded with contract offers. Jason Siegel, an Austin-based artists' agent, called while we were at our last fair, in Omaha. Over lunch soon after our return, Jason explained his position in the art market and his belief in emerging artists. He was going into a new venture in the art publishing business and planned to open a gallery in Austin.

At first I had doubts about Jason—he seemed too young, perhaps lacking the savvy to maneuver in the sophisticated art market. I didn't want to make a mistake that would send me back to the local guild shows. Al and I mulled over Jason's offer for hours after the luncheon. Al felt that over the last several years we had taken many chances with our lives, and that we should therefore take a chance on someone who was taking the risk of moving in a new direction. I polled my friends. My brother Larry, bless his heart, reminded me that my heroes Degas and Renoir had had the same agent throughout their entire careers. Claudia thought it was better to have an enthusiastic agent than one who was more established but perhaps complacent. The consensus seemed to be that going with our instincts would serve me best.

As soon as we made the decision, Jason took two of my paintings, doubled the price, and sold them to his clients the same day. We have never had a written contract with Jason, but over the years our friendship and our trust in each other has grown. He suggested to Al that while he was establishing his gallery, I get some gallery exposure on my own. Al, always eager to tell the world about me, immediately turned his attention to finding me a gallery. Once again, my life was about to change.

CHAPTER EIGHT

THE BLIND ARTIST

*Painting is a blind man's profession. He
paints not what he sees, but what he feels,
what he tells himself he has seen.*

—PABLO PICASSO

IN JUNE 1999, Al and I had a surprise twenty-fifth wedding anniversary celebration. The surprise wasn't just the party we hadn't even suspected, with fabulous Cajun food and cake and music, cards and goofy gifts. The revelation was that we had so many friends who cared about us. Intimate friendships and community had crept up on us, a delightful by-product of the humanizing process our situation had forced upon us. The best present of all.

The only thing in life that still scares me is that something terrible will happen to Al. But he promises me that I will die first, and he's never broken a promise. Being with Al is like being bathed in a warm waterfall, like being enveloped in a sable coat. Losing Al is the one thing that could put me over the edge. I worry that if I lost Al I wouldn't be able to control the demons that are always lurking at the edge of my mind, waiting to take over.

I often think that the real miracle of my life is my marriage to Al. But our relationship certainly didn't start out as a match made in heaven. We met in 1973 in a debate class at the University of South Carolina, arguing vehemently on opposite sides of some now forgotten issue. Al was a midshipman assigned to the staff at the university naval ROTC center, studying psychology. I was studying nursing, trying to escape my odious first husband and learn a trade that would support me. In total rebellion mode, I was dating ten guys, even though I hadn't yet filed for divorce, and living in a forty-dollar-a-month tenement apartment with four other women.

Al had a home and a brand-new 1972 Monte Carlo. He was living with one of my girlfriends, but they fought all the time— he ran a tight ship and she was a slob. She wanted to date one of my boyfriends, and he wanted to date me. I can't say we ever officially dated, though. He just doggedly pursued me, and I tried to stay a step ahead of him. I'd come home from a date, and he'd be waiting on the doorstep. So we'd go out to Big Boy and have strawberry pie or some dinner. Al says that today he'd be called a stalker. He claims he fell for me right away, but at that point I looked at Al simply as someone who could feed me and help take care of my economic needs. A few months later, when I couldn't cover the rent and tuition, he made me an offer I couldn't refuse. "Why don't you move in with me? There are more rats than people at your house."

So I moved in and he paid my tuition and bought me a car. No candy or flowers; he knew better than to try to romance me. A year passed, and I was still married and attending school. I still assumed that living with Al was just a temporary situation until my divorce came through. When Al finished his degree in 1974 and was being shipped to Newport, Rhode Island, he asked me to marry him. My divorce was final, but I had a year to go for my nursing degree, and I didn't want to remarry, ever. Al persisted, reasoning that if we were married I'd receive his naval benefits even if he were sent back to Vietnam.

Al's mother had recently been in an automobile accident and could not come to South Carolina, so off we went to New York to get married. We arrived in Queens to discover that his mother had already planned the wedding—for later that day. Cake, flowers, food, license, a superior court judge, family, and friends were ready and waiting. Somehow his mother had managed to dig up my father and his girlfriend. Seeing my father sent me into a tailspin, reminding me that I should never have married the first time around. An hour before the noon ceremony, I called off the wedding. Al drove me to the beach in Oyster Bay, Long Island, and pleaded with me to reconsider. Finally he got me to acquiesce; at six o'clock on June 29 we were married. Everyone had waited around for the ceremony, sustained by copious rations of food and drink. At two A.M. we drove into Manhattan with a contingency of revelers in our wake. One of our wedding presents was a night in the Americana Hotel, where I promptly lost my wedding ring. So you can see how it all began.

During our first year of marriage, I stayed in South Carolina while Al lived in Newport. Somehow this pattern of living apart continued through our fifteenth year of marriage. We would move together to Al's next posting only to have jobs, schooling, or circumstances force us to live apart. Finally a permanent posting to Houston gave us stability. We've been together ever since.

What kept us together in those early years was that Al adored me and put up with a lot of high drama. Heaven knows why. I didn't trust that anyone could truly love me, and I had to keep testing this love. I hated feeling vulnerable, and I had no idea how to respond to someone who actually cared for me, who wasn't with me out of obligation. Disconnected from my own emotions, I counted on Al to create my happiness. One memorable argument escalated to the point where I stormed off and locked myself in our garage, and Al came out and broke the door down. Can you imagine? I wanted to feel something, so I provoked Al into providing the emotional juice. I remember standing in the kitchen and smiling to myself because I figured his intense emotional response must mean that he really loved me. Now that I have easy access to my feelings, I don't need to steal them from anyone else.

Our first fifteen years together were like a passionate, ill-starred love affair, punctuated by my runaway episodes and spiced up by almost annual postings to new locations. In the calm interludes, we lived a rather typical good life. I did my thing and Al did his. We each had our own pals, our own interests and activities. We traveled together and, because of our frequent moves, there were always new adventures, new vistas, new people to entertain us. Marriage didn't get stale. We were a two-income couple with sufficient money to live well, to vacation, and to acquire any new toys we favored. Al was a homebody who liked his creature comforts, his cars and collectibles. He always made us a comfortable nest. I just liked the freedom.

When my vision began to fail, Al said he felt like he'd lost an arm. All of a sudden I couldn't go places and do the things we enjoyed. We were both so independent, and now we could no longer go our separate ways. Life as we knew it—our comfortable, predictable life—was over. We had never actually had to care for each other. Now caretaking was at the core of our relationship, first with my blindness, then with Al's heart attack and strokes. These major, life-altering crises could not be ignored. Many times Al and I thought divorce would be the simplest solution. We hovered for months on the brink of separation, each believing that divorce would clean our emotional closet of rage and blame.

Emotional baggage, however, follows you wherever you go. To incorporate changes in our physical status, in our everyday freedoms, in our self-image, we had to unpack and downsize. We faced the real possibility that one or both of us might suddenly die. Patience, forbearance, empathy, and tolerance were not our forte. We were proficient at anger, indifference, and self-centeredness. We had to give them up. We were pushed to change not only our behavior but our perspective on life.

We barely survived this emotional turmoil. But our seemingly insurmountable crisis made us realize how important we were to each other. Our willingness, however grudging at first, to rise to the challenge of caring for each other led to a deep and abiding love. We discovered that our happiness was interdependent and mirrored in the emotional effort we invested in the relationship.

It has often occurred to me that without Al's health crisis, I might never have done what was necessary to deal with my vision loss. Getting myself on a plane and flying to California saved both our lives. In twenty years of marriage, I had never really considered that I loved Al and could lose him. Now I actually like him, too. Al says that we were two miserable people, living alone together, who practically had to be destroyed to get what we have now. Today we both believe that the crises we faced were a blessing. I truly feel that unless something drastic had come along to shake us out of our frozen complacency, we wouldn't be together today.

In 1998, following Jason's suggestion, Al set out to find me a gallery. It didn't take long. On the July Fourth weekend, we were at the Garland Star-Spangled Fourth fair, outside of Dallas, where I'd been invited to mount an exhibit of my paintings as a guest artist. There Jeff Crilley, a reporter from the local Fox affiliate, "discovered" the amazing blind painter who'd been showing and selling her work all over the country. This was the first time I enjoyed being interviewed. Maybe I'd let down my habitual defenses for once, but Jeff seemed truly interested in my work, not just my blindness. He actually wanted to know how I develop a new composition and choose my subjects. We talked at length about the methods I employ to transfer images in my mind to the canvas. I thought the piece Jeff put together managed to be both insightful and inspirational, rather than the usual "Omigod, the artist is blind."

As soon as the story aired on Fox in Dallas that night, we started getting phone calls and e-mails from viewers in the area. At the fair the next day, I was deluged with people who were genuinely interested in my work. Their questions, too, were not just "Why are you painting?" They wanted to know what inspired my paintings, how I choose colors, and how I learned to draw and paint. The news spot was so well received that the reporter syndicated his piece to all the Fox stations and sold it to CNN. At various points during our travels, local reporters had found the story of the blind painter good copy for the local media, and I'd done many radio interviews. But this was the story that made a splash. Overnight, I was besieged with reporters and art collectors demanding to know more.

It all happened very fast. Within the month, I was offered a show at the Austin Museum of Art. The exhibitions director needed someone to fill in at the last minute for a scheduled exhibition that had been canceled. Several small pieces sold within the first few weeks of the show, at prices up to two thousand dollars. I was euphoric. Then Al found the opportunity he'd been waiting for. Searching for a gallery willing to take a chance on an up-and-coming artist, he made an appointment to visit the Florence Art Gallery in Dallas. While he was showing my paintings to the gallery owner, the art critic from the *Dallas Morning News* happened by. He was taken with the paintings and wanted an interview the same day. Al asked the gallery owner if we could hold the interview there. Right then the gallery decided to add me to their stable of artists. Now I was represented by one of the most prestigious art galleries in Texas. My paintings would hang alongside work by world-famous artists.

In November 1998, riding a wave of media publicity about my unique talents, the Florence Art Gallery in Dallas opened Wonders of the Mind's Eye. I got all dolled up in a basic black dress Al and I had picked out the day before. It was the first time in two years I wasn't wearing paint-splattered clothes, and the first time I spoke to a large group.

The opening was, as they say, a media frenzy! It was standing room only in the cavernous gallery. Outside, an overflow crowd tried to push its way in, anxious to see the work of the blind artist. There were film crews and reporters from both local and national stations, all scrambling to get an interview.

The show sold out in the first hour. Usually dignified art patrons fought over the limited supply of paintings, pulling them from the walls in order to buy them before someone else could lay claim. I was astonished to overhear reporters gathered around a collector who had just paid six thousand dollars for one of my watercolors.

It was tremendously exciting. I had dreamt of this media blitz. I had pictured myself charging out into the world with my paintbrush, changing public opinion about people with disabilities, creating breathtaking murals, and marching the streets without a cane. Here was the fulfillment of my dream of an art angel (like you see in the movies) becoming a patron and launching my career. Fantasies multiplied on the blank screen of my mind. I would write and illustrate a children's book and give the proceeds to children's hospitals and other charities. I would climb Mount Everest (which I later decided would be easier than trying to make it in the art world). One of my paintings would hang at the National Gallery. It was all happening! Returning to earth, to real life at my real opening, I found that people were intrigued by what I had to say about painting. They seemed fascinated to hear how my approach to life and painting differed from theirs. I stayed at the gallery answering questions late into the night.

I explained to my audience that my motives and objectives in painting are quite different from those of a sighted artist. A sighted artist wants to interpret what he or she sees, to develop a style and a vision and then refine it over time. I have practical needs. What I learn from painting I translate into my ability to apprehend the world outside my door. If I can organize the lines and shapes on a canvas, and keep them from overlapping or intersecting in an unnatural way, I can walk more safely to the corner and find my way to the ladies' room. I can avoid knocking over the lamp on Al's desk. Painting makes the world more concrete. It keeps me sane and grounded. I paint to keep my memories of the world alive, and to help me solidify the present-time world I apprehend through my remaining senses.

I don't repeat the same subject, trying to perfect my ability to capture it. I paint something new with each canvas. Repetition does not help me document the world. Once a task is learned, repetition does not enhance or improve my ability to keep my internal filing cabinet of images up to date. Increasingly often, I am converting to visual imagery the world

I take in through my other senses—hearing and touch and smell. I paint a kind of multisensory *ambience.*

Yes, I paint for pure pleasure, to entertain myself and my audience. But it is more important to me that my viewers understand my world. The reassurance that I am still connected to the reality of the sighted is paramount in my work. Painting is my way of expressing who I am and what I know. Feedback from viewers is my way of ascertaining that my inner world has resonance in the outer world of the sighted. My question is, "What are you seeing, and is your reality the same as mine?"

That night at the gallery, I went on to say that I live with a chronic degenerative disease and am ever aware of the limited minutes remaining on my life's clock, of my vulnerability and precarious presence on this earth. Like a diary, my paintings record my life. Painting places me squarely on the path of life in the present moment. On this path I have the freedom to accept my fate, to adapt and change. My art is a microcosm of these moments of change and adaptation. In the world of my painting studio, my mind is always occupied, intent on something difficult and challenging and life affirming. I am keeping the doubts and demons at bay. I am not afraid. When I am painting I am the happiest person alive, and when I am not I am blind. Necessity is the real mother of my inventions. If I could see, I confessed to my audience, I wouldn't paint.

The *Today* show filmed at the gallery for eight hours on the day of the opening gala. The producer confided that she had not experienced such an exciting opening since Andrew Wyeth released his new works several years earlier. She called it "a mystical experience." *Today*'s crew arranged to come to my home and studio in Georgetown the following week for an in-depth interview, and more filming. The plan was to air my story over the course of a week, five minutes a day. The fantasies escalated: this was the big-time; this meant nationwide recognition. I might land a prominent New York gallery.

Alas, my high-flying fantasies started crashing to earth almost as fast as I dreamed them up. I soon sensed a dark undercurrent. I got the drift of what was going on when they asked me to touch someone's face and then draw it on-camera for them. They were upset when I explained that this was not how I worked. "Who cuts your meat?" they wanted to know. "How do you get to the bathroom without assistance?" "Why do your eyes follow the movements of whoever is speaking to you?" The subtext was "Are you *really* blind?" The interviewers seemed disappointed that I lived in a comfortable home and could actually function fairly independently. My friend Sylvia said I shouldn't have worn my diamond jewelry to the opening. Claudia said the *Today* show would have preferred a street urchin. My fantasies took a nosedive when they checked with my doctors to confirm the depth of my blindness and got them to sign affidavits. A producer phoned my social worker to find out why someone might pretend to be blind. What was the economic benefit to Lisa, they wanted to know, to pretend to be a blind painter? What did she expect to gain from perpetuating this hoax? The answer, of course, is that no amount of money can compensate for living in my world. There are no advantages to being blind or deaf or in any way disabled.

I put up with their interrogation, I'm embarrassed to admit. I wanted to be on the *Today* show. It was part of my dream. But the next time I heard from them they told me that they were putting the spot on the shelf "for the time being." So, for the time being, I tried to hope for the best.

The morning after the opening-night gala, we went out and bought all the newspapers to check the reviews. Most were flattering, rave notices. Almost all. The gallery owner was dismayed to find a review criticizing the gallery for "exploiting the handicapped and children." *Children? Am I that short?* The critic hadn't attended the opening or visited the gallery. His critique had nothing to say about the art itself, the runaway sales, or the positive reactions at the gala—only that the gallery was exploiting my blindness. Upset by the review, the owner was uncertain as to whether "our relationship" should continue.

At the time of my exhibition, the Florence Gallery was showing predominantly abstract art. Eager to exhibit my growing facility with figurative subjects, I painted a series of contemporary dance pieces. When Al delivered these paintings to the gallery, the owner said she would be embarrassed to show them to her friends and clients. "Every artist knows that figurative paintings don't sell," she added.

New to the "legitimate" art market, ignorant of the practices in the business, I had no idea that galleries tend to specialize in particular styles or periods, and cater to specific clientele. Perhaps the problem with my figurative paintings offered the gallery a graceful exit, given the owner's concern about "exploiting the blind." In any case, thus ended my relationship with the Florence Gallery. It ended badly, but I have one momentous memory of the Florence Gallery experience. After the opening, I walked around a city block by myself for the first time since losing my sight.

I was learning fast that the art world operates under a bizarre code of ethics and taste. It's a cutthroat business. Typically a gallery takes a 50 to 70 percent commission for your work. You have to do your own framing, and sometimes even cover the publicity and opening costs. Often a gallery will have the gall to not pay you on time. Galleries also, despite their professed interest in creativity, seek conformity. They want to represent someone whose painting style is popular, or whose work resembles an artist whose work is selling well. For example, if a gallery knows that trees sell, they *highly* encourage you to paint trees. Al and I recently toured the galleries in Santa Fe, at times eavesdropping on the customers' conversations. "Mark, doesn't that artist remind you of the one, you know, who we saw in Scottsdale last year?" we heard. "I know it's not the same name, but I really liked her style and they are so similar." Back then, I hadn't paid attention to these messages. I do now, and I'm glad I do not paint the same café or vase of flowers over and over again just to satisfy some gallery.

It felt as if I'd been punched in the gut when Al brought my new paintings home. I took it personally, still sure that art was me and I was my paintings. But I was bored with abstract painting, and I'd discovered that I could not stop the images of people flooding my mind. Ballerinas prancing across my field of inner vision, old men on park benches reminiscing, musicians wailing in smoky jazz clubs, and children on swings clamored to be painted. Prior to losing my sight, I'd had little empathy for or curiosity about other people's lives. Now I couldn't get enough of people's voices and stories, couldn't help imagining how they appeared and interacted with one another. I wanted to know their feelings and paint their emotions. I'm awed by the breadth and depth of the human experience, and by the singular qualities of each person. This uniqueness is what I try to paint. The human body is a mystery of planes. It is the nuanced combining of these planes, the subtleties of symmetry and fluidity of motion, that produces the one-of-a-kind human body. Even so, the unique combination of line, shape, and form do not add up to making the individual recognizable on the canvas. For me, the struggle is to impart each figure with a distinctive life energy.

Certain that the rejected Florence Gallery paintings would sell, Al decided to create a one-page Web site and market them on the Internet. He spent two solid months learning how to design and publish Web sites. Finally the site went live and I began selling the figurative watercolor paintings. The first month www.lisafittipaldi.com was online I sold four of the dance-series paintings rejected by the Florence Gallery for double what I would have received from the gallery. The most noteworthy of this series is titled *Impulse;* it's a bright-hued acrylic and watercolor on canvas depicting a line of overlapping dancers suspended on the canvas in various ballet poses. *Impulse* was my first painting of multiple action figures showing facial expression and emotion. I was so afraid to lose the mental image that I completed painting *Impulse* in one fifty-six-hour marathon session. Probably because of its complexity, *Impulse* became one of my most controversial and sought-after paintings, and a successful print edition. Within the year, the painting was featured in numerous newspapers, magazines, and television shows. *Impulse* was later purchased by a prominent art collector.

There are many techniques for applying watercolors. The artist can work wet on wet, use a dry-brush technique, or apply the wet paint on a dry surface. My method is to build up thin layers of color. But watercolor is not a forgiving medium. It requires a decisive approach to the brushstroke, design, and color chosen. Once the brush strikes the paper, the results are fixed, and they are not easily correctable. Overwork the paper, add too little or too much water, and you'll ruin the painting. Watercolor, like life, demands a commitment.

Without a strong composition, a painting will never quite work. Weeks before beginning a painting, I've already made many mental corrections and adjustments to my inner vision. Finally I draw the composition on the watercolor paper, using a metallic silver pencil so I can feel the lines. Early on, I employed complex strategies for orienting myself to the paper. I would place grids of string at various intervals along the length and width of the paper, a simple geometry that let me know more or less where I was. When I moved to San Antonio and began oil painting, I relied on staples placed around the frame of the canvas. I marked the center of the canvas with a small acrylic dot. This reference point permitted me to adjust my composition by counting the spaces on an invisible grid. I no longer need such guidelines. I rely completely on my internal picture of the image to reposition the lines of my drawing on the paper or canvas.

Adding color to the painting is the final stage. My intellectual knowledge of color theory and properties makes my colors clean and vibrant, "untainted" by what the eye would see. I was unable to keep my colors clear using the traditional color-wheel palette. What worked for me was a rectangular porcelain butcher's pan. I place the red in one corner of my palette, the yellow in another, and blue in a third. An imaginary triangle forms where, in the pan's center, I mix the desired color. Even when I'm careful, I throw out a lot of paint in order to keep the colors pure.

When I worked in watercolor, I used only the primary colors: red, yellow, and blue. The difference in granularity, texture, and weight of the primary colors enabled me to distinguish each color by touch, and automatically develop the color mixes

I desired. Watercolor uses the bare paper for white. I never use paint directly from the tube. I mix a warm black, a cool black, or a blue-black, based on hue, value, and tonal qualities. A warm black, for example, can be created by mixing alizarin crimson and Windsor green. I understand how light striking the canvas changes the appearance of colors, and how shading creates the illusion of dimension. As my technical abilities strengthen, so too does my ability to employ what I have learned about color theory. I want the canvas to sparkle and shimmer with color.

For all my love of color, there is no color in my internal imagery, and very little black-gray-white variation. Everything in my visual field is the white of a snowstorm, or the icy blue-gray of sleet. It seems that when I lost my ability to perceive color, I lost my ability to close my eyes and re-create a color. I know intellectually that lemons are yellow, but I cannot picture yellow. And yes, the sky is blue, but I have no concrete way of describing blue. I know because of the strict lineup of my materials that a tube of paint is cadmium red, but I have only an intellectual knowledge of the difference between cadmium red and alizarin crimson.

I have devoted whole months to studying the properties of individual pigments. I know, for example, that cadmium yellow light is a clean, strong, opaque yellow, whereas cadmium yellow medium and cadmium yellow deep have a bright yellow-orange base. Technically, these pigments differ on the color index and in their chemical classifications. Knowing that diarylide yellows have a slight greenish base and are either transparent or semi-opaque helps me to understand just how one will combine with a naphthol red, which has a red-violet base. I am not influenced by the visual appearance of a particular color; rather, I combine pigments according to the specific formulas I've learned to achieve the desired final effect. Where the sighted painter applies the paint to the canvas, then evaluates the outcome and makes corrections, I apply color with the intention of reaching a predetermined outcome.

Over time, my technical and intellectual mastery of color theory has led somehow to an instinctive use of color in my painting. When I work with color, I am on some other plane. I glaze one color over another, sometimes obscuring the lines and creating new edges, trusting some combination of my deep knowledge and deep sensing.

Finally I sign the painting. It shows how far I've come that at first I couldn't even write my signature, so I signed my paintings with a thumbprint. Today my signature combines longhand and Braille.

I may have been rejected by the Florence Gallery and put on hold by the *Today* show, but the "amazing blind painter" story hadn't abated. Al and I were beginning to feel invaded by press attention we no longer wanted. We began to argue about whether or not to give interviews, whether it was a good idea to cooperate with inquisitive journalists. Whereas once Al had welcomed all publicity, he was getting the message that not all news coverage is good news coverage.

All the attention meant that my work was in great demand. I was establishing a much broader base of collectors. My prices rose, and I had immediate buyers for my work. I was offered solo gallery and museum shows. The downside was that—yet again—all my insecurities and doubts came rushing back to haunt me. With so much of the focus on the "blind painter," I was right back to wondering whether I was a decent artist or a sideshow act. Were collectors buying my work on its own merits, or were they buying because I was blind? Was my work any good? Were my paintings, as I desperately wanted to believe, the worthy confluence of my intellectual prowess, my dedication, my years of study, my talent and sheer hard work? Every possible doubt about my abilities, along with every recollection of my painful past, was still slamming around in my head. My own torments were not helped by a new chorus of doubters and naysayers who sprung up in the wake of all this attention. "Well, fine," they said, "but you're not really an artist if you don't paint landscapes." Then it was "Why do you paint so many different subjects?"

True to form, every time a new doubt arose, I'd go back to chanting my old mantra, *I'll show you*. I'd trudge back into my studio, muttering under my breath as I doggedly mastered the next level of my painting. "See, I can paint a landscape." To which the comeback was "Yes, but your figures don't have recognizable faces." *Right*. Real artists can do that. Back I'd go to the studio. I've since learned that not many sighted artists are adept at rendering the human figure.

The question of whether I was faking blindness lingered. I often heard, "Well, she must still have some vision." People are always trying to quantify blindness, to pocket the experience for their own understanding. I try to explain that there is a broad range of vision impairment and blindness. Most blind people do not live in total darkness. Depending on the vision problem, a blind person may be able to perform one task but not another comparable task. A person with macular degeneration may have difficulty reading or recognizing faces but be able to move around easily using their peripheral vision. Also, by the way, most blind people do not have extrasensory powers or extraordinary musical talent.

In my case, I'd explain, I am really quite blind, full-on blind; it's like a snow globe in here. Nothing would convince the doubters, though, and I played right into their hands. If I'd have been more confident, these responses wouldn't have cut me so deeply. Though I would have denied it, I was still painting for approval and acceptance. Against all logic, I was trying to show the world that I was no different from any other artist. *Sure.* It's true that in painting I was finding a way to navigate the world, but the driving force behind the long hours in the studio was still *I'll prove that I can do what you say is impossible. I'll show you.* In my mind's eye, my paintings worked. But I had no way of proving their value to myself. I needed the validation of the sighted, although, to add to the confusion, I mistrusted even those who profusely praised me.

The irony is that I can no longer paint landscapes. Even my photographic memory and the daily diligence of painting have not staved off the relentless erosion of the visible world. When we drove to Utah last year, Al rhapsodized about the scenery along the way—tumbleweed, sand dunes, rock outcroppings, a mackerel sky. Most of it no longer means a word to me, but his enjoyment was contagious, and I think my questions probed him to see things he might not otherwise have noticed. Slowly my personal universe has shrunk to what I can keep alive through my remaining senses. I cannot touch what is on a high shelf in my kitchen, much less the vast panorama of landscape. Even a tree, because it is not immediately relevant to my life, is now an abstract concept. I have no way of putting a face on those I've met since I went blind. I know them by voice, scent, and their ineffable energy, and that's what I paint. Faces I once knew well are now vague memory traces. My bed and chair, my brushes and easel, my husband's body, and the twenty-two cane sweeps of my driveway are clear and solid. But the world beyond my sidewalk is slowly dissolving.

Just about this time, at the height of my confusion about my legitimacy as a painter, the *Today* show producer called. "We just can't run the segment," she began. "It's simply not believable." As I listened with my heart in my throat, she went on to reassure me that my work was marvelous. But they could not overcome their skepticism. My guess is that I didn't fit the picture. I didn't do the Stevie Wonder act, being led around on someone's arm, clacking my cane as I went. The storyboard they had devised was different from my life. My story wouldn't tug their viewers' heartstrings.

The Florence Gallery dismissal and the final *Today* show rejection were like a one-two punch. Shattered, I went back to bed. My self-worth was still inextricably tangled up with my painting—in particular, others' evaluation of my painting. For all the small, slow steps I was taking in the direction of self-reliance and self-motivation, I still defined myself through others.

All my life I'd measured my worth by my productivity. If I couldn't validate my worth through the sale of my paintings without constant challenges to my capabilities and my veracity, the hell with it, I decided. Why should I continue to paint? By this time I had less than 2 percent blurry central vision. The official classification was "nonfunctional," or less than 20/1,000 vision. I had never seen my figurative paintings. In a "Why bother?" funk of rejection, I told myself that I'd learned all I needed from painting. Inconsolable, I began yet another descent into the abyss that still threatened to claim me.

I really tortured myself this time around. Naturally, I asked myself the classic self-pitying question: "Why me?" Television aired other bizarre and unbelievable stories, so why not mine? What did I do wrong that I was unworthy of the *Today* show? I'd tried so hard to do everything right. I'd learned to be independent. I knew how to dress myself. I'd learned Braille . . . sort of. Didn't I deserve a pat on the back? If I was truly an artist, and not a freak show, wasn't that enough for the *Today* show? On and on I ranted, hurt and angry, crying crocodile tears, trying to sooth my fragile ego.

The *Today* show rejection was the low-water mark of my battle to ride the wave of recognition without sinking my ship of self-confidence. It still haunts me. Here I was trying to be the best blind person, a great painter, but the perfect blind-person skills in which I took such pride were being used against me. I'd worked so hard to adapt to the world of the sighted, going beyond my disability to adjust to a world that cannot adapt to me. I felt I had something to say to those in the sighted world. I believed that I had unique perceptual insights for artists and designers. I could not understand why the media wanted to perpetuate misconceptions of the blind as not merely sightless but socially and mentally impaired as well. I should have been expending all that emotional energy painting new pictures, but it was a long time before I achieved a more grown-up perspective.

Now I had my art studio and nothing to paint, nowhere to go, and nothing to do except bemoan my fate. Then out of the blue I was contacted by Health Communications, asking me to illustrate the third in a series of children's books called *Chicken Soup for Little Souls*. The theme of the story was symbiosis and possibilities. The protagonists were a blind boy and a sighted girl who wanted to ride in a bike race, even though she had a broken leg. Looking for fresh ideas, the publisher had chosen me because I was a fine artist rather than an illustrator. Not to mention that it was a publicist's dream, a book about a blind person illustrated by a blind person!

I signed the contract. Without the foggiest clue as to what I was doing, I went ahead and began the work. But I had no concept of the difficulty involved in reproducing a watercolor painting in print or, for that matter, what actually constituted a book illustration. Little did I know that they wanted my paintings to utilize the same colors as the first two books in the series, and to somehow coordinate with their style. No one communicated these issues until I sent them the completed plates.

Then problems arose. They began faxing examples of what they wanted the cover to look like so I could see an example. *Excuse me?* Then they complained that I had not used the same shade of red or blue as the other illustrators (who had, by the way, worked in acrylic paint). In sheer frustration I snapped at the editor, "I'm blind, don't you get it? I can't see your damn blue!" Al, ever my champion, insisted that the publisher at least pay for my time and the initial plates. Although the book never made it into print, I was compensated for my efforts.

My usual response would have been to go into my swoon and refuse to paint ever again. But I was learning that danger awaits me when I don't paint. Anyone who has had horrible things happen to them is prey to bleak internal fears. If my mind isn't occupied with the problems of painting, it sometimes fills with images of things I know I haven't seen, and I become anxious and frightened. I don't know where they come from, and I don't welcome them. The idea that I might be able to create images from a prior world is worse than being in the dark. A photographer friend who stopped by last year casually remarked that my new painting of a group of men at a counter looked exactly like a photograph he'd seen that was taken in 1929. It scared me so much that I didn't paint for two months.

Every day that I don't paint my despair deepens and I become more agitated and depressed. I'm desperate to escape, but since I don't drink or use drugs, and I can't drive a car or jump on a plane, I can't just zone out. I have to proactively distract myself. Now I have a ten-minute rule, which is simply that when I get like this, I must do *anything* for ten minutes. Wash my brushes. Fold the laundry. Dance around to some music. Walk outside and get the mail. It was finally dawning on me that giving up painting again didn't seem to be the answer. But at this point I didn't know what was.

My health problems were getting worse, and I wasn't doing a great job of addressing them. They weren't going away. Living successfully with any chronic disease (all autoimmune disorders are chronic) is based on your ability to cope—physically, mentally, spiritually, and psychically. I had to learn the hard way to take a proactive attitude toward dealing with my health, and I spent many hours on the Internet researching vasculitis. Johns Hopkins and Cleveland Clinics have vasculitis centers to study this disease, which manifests itself in so many forms, and I keep up with their findings. Having gone through life dealing with health problems, I'm not intimidated by the medical profession. By now I know as much as my physicians do about vasculitis. I understand why the medical community is frustrated with its inability to cure or control the symptoms of this baffling disease.

Vasculitis had taken away my sight, limited my ability to eat a variety of foods, created uncontrollable asthma, compromised my heart, and manifested itself as eczema, hives, and kidney disease. It had provoked anaphylactic reactions to antibiotics. Now it was in the process of destroying my hearing—another warning that I had to get serious about taking care of my health and my so-called life.

PART III

RETURN

CHAPTER NINE

COURSE CORRECTION

Art is not a mirror held up to reality,
but a hammer with which to shape it.

—BERTOLDT BRECHT

So WHAT WAS I TO DO if I wasn't painting? Besides sulking? The problem was that I was fast losing my ability to sulk. I'd try to wail and lament my fate, but I couldn't really work myself up for it anymore. There was an internal battle going on for my sanity and sense of humor—and the sulking was losing.

My negativity and resistance had competition now. Something was percolating inside me—a hard-won confidence, a growing self-awareness, a fuller sense of life's possibilities. Almost imperceptibly, I was emerging from my prolonged fugue of depression and anger. You need fuel to keep the fire of anger going, and in my case the fuel was evaporating. I could no longer convince myself that no one cared about me or understood me, or that my life was meaningless. I had too much evidence to the contrary. Clearly, blaming the world for my unhappiness wasn't working. Having spent four years doing a bang-up job of being angry, obnoxious, and resistant to change, I (and anyone who tried to get near me) was more miserable than ever. I would have to look inside myself to bank the fires of my rage. My desolation was hurting me most of all, and I was not suicidal.

People change only when they are forced to change. Fear makes us cling to our known baggage, however awful, rather than jettison it in the hope of lightening our load. But what you are saying when you cling to your sinking life raft is "I'm afraid. I don't trust myself." I have a girlfriend who has breast cancer, and she is so angry that it radiates from her pores. Her barely disguised rage is so palpable that you don't want to be in the same room with her. Her doctor says she has a 95 percent chance of survival, but her interpretation is "There's a time bomb in there." I've been there; I recognize her terror.

It's not surprising that when I first began to let down my defenses, the paralyzing grief that I'd long avoided replaced my anger. Finally the tears came, carried on wave upon wave of sorrow. When I emerged from the exhaustion of grieving, it was as if I'd gone through an exorcism. The changes were so internal I didn't notice them until they worked their way to the surface and started showing up in my behavior. Wonder of wonders, I was becoming a better friend to my friends, a more compassionate person, a better spouse, a more diverse and interesting human being. Someone fascinated by life's marvels, yearning for human connection and a place in the community.

There is no map that gets you from anger and depression to inner peace and contentment. When I look back over the years to try to understand how these changes came about, I see that it was a barely perceptible procession of incremental changes, quiet, ordinary, unglamorous gestures that abraded the surface to expose a kinder, gentler me. Beneath the radar of my awareness, the years of being helped and comforted, the years of discipline and study were taking effect. Only in the heartbeats between very quiet moments is it possible to recognize that a passage is being made into another life. However adamant my resistance, there came the reluctant admission that I had no alternative but to adapt to my circumstances. The question of "Why me?" morphed into "What do I need to know?" and "What will work for me?" and "How do I go about getting there?" I saw that I would have to fix all the parts of me that were broken, ineffective, and inappropriate. A tall order.

There were a few notable stepping-stones along the path. One, of course, was the child's watercolor set that Al had flung onto my bed so many years ago. Another was the refuge I'd found in music, beginning with a friend's gift of Sibelius's moving Symphony No. 1. Books on tape and reader services for the blind helped compensate for the loss of the written word. A computer program reopened the information highway, linking me to the Internet and the wider world.

A painful phone call was pivotal. Late one night, desperately seeking connection and consolation, I worked up the nerve to call someone I hadn't spoken with for twenty-five years, a woman I'd known during a wretched period I'd tried to forget. I telephoned to apologize for my emotional distance and shallowness, for my inability to offer her comfort during her tumultuous first marriage. I hoped to get some insight into that unhappy time. Most of all, I wanted to cry and weep and let my hair down to someone who was now, really, a stranger—and therefore safe.

Ten minutes into our conversation she interrupted. "With all you've been through," she said, "I can't believe you haven't changed." I was stunned. Hadn't my struggle with blindness altered my perceptions and my ability to sympathize?

"Not as far as I can tell," she snapped. "Actually, you sound exactly like your mother. Curious, isn't it? She was judgmental, and so are you."

I had been railing on about the absurd questions people ask about my blindness, the insensitive and crass way I'm treated.

Here it was her fiftieth birthday; she was diabetic and living on a fixed income, processing through another awful divorce, and I was ranting and raving because people were taking an interest in me, showing enough concern to ask me about my blindness, however awkwardly.

Okay, I get it. At that moment I realized that it was a gift to be forced to change, to appreciate rather than denigrate, to analyze what you need to survive, and to find the internal fortitude to take the steps to change. Change required me to consider and understand another person's perspective and, conversely, become less self-centered. It took years for me to admit the errors of my ways, to drop my defensiveness and negativity. But that phone call was a marker on the path.

Years later, we talked again. She called in the middle of the night, sobbing, in a state of emotional terror. This time I listened to her story, and did not interrupt or anticipate the outcome. In the middle of the conversation she said, "Fine. I am done" and hung up. Two weeks later a pair of Tweety Bird socks arrived in the mail, with a short unsigned note. "Sorry," it said. "You are not like your mother at all."

When you cannot see, you have no choice but to trust others' motives, their goodwill and basic human decency—every minute of every day. I was ignorant, a rank novice, in the trust department. I had spent my whole life building walls of self-sufficiency and self-protection so that I wouldn't have to depend on anyone else for anything. Suspicious, skeptical, paranoid, that was me. Terrified of shame or embarrassment, I worked hard to do everything perfectly. I was a well-defended citadel of competence and solvency. I needed nothing from others. I gave nothing and expected nothing in return. Given my childhood, I had every reason to defend my borders, and I had done it well. When blindness knocked on my door, I could no more allow people to help me than I could navigate myself down the hall to the bathroom. *Surrender* was not a word in my vocabulary. If I take the view that everything happens for a reason, I would have to say that if your problem is trust, going blind is probably the number one solution.

Today, I can say that intimate friendships have been one of the great blessings of losing my sight, and my friends are probably a good barometer of my progress. I am reminded daily, by a moment of laughter with Nora or a quick phone call to Jennifer, that I am truly cared about, that affection has come into my life as a direct result of my blindness. Each of my close friends is different, but they all share a zest for life, a desire to engage with the world, a willingness to change and improve. My good friends don't make allowances for my blindness, and they don't hesitate to call me on the carpet when I'm out of line or expecting special treatment. Believe me, I test them at times. I can call my friend Claudia at two in the morning, and she'll say, "Hi, what's up?," aware that I don't distinguish between night and day. Or she'll call me to ask if I'm okay this week, and I'll say, "Yep, I'm fine. Good-bye."

After a lifetime of keeping my pain and troubles to myself, I tell Claudia everything. Of course, this works only because she does the same with me. She's not playing therapist. Sometimes I don't see my friend Peg for six months, but then we'll be on the phone for hours, which is pretty remarkable, because I hate the telephone. One time Niki called to ask how I was doing. "Uhh . . ." I began, and she was at my house in twenty minutes. Lately I've learned to call my friends when I'm in need, instead of moping around hoping that someone will figure out that I'm in trouble.

I have my bleak days, when I dare not paint for fear that the darkness will bleed onto the canvas. That's when I'll put in an "I desperately need you" call to a friend to come and distract me. A couple of months ago, I just fell apart. I couldn't stop crying for twenty-four hours, which is not like me. Our bed-and-breakfast was full of guests. Everyone wanted a piece of me, and I could barely get out of bed. Al's memory losses had put him in vacation mode, and he was *out to lunch*. I couldn't hear for about six hours, and every minute of silence terrified me. I had bronchitis, and my asthma was so bad I should have been in the hospital, but I'd refused to go. They had upped my chemotherapy, and I was nauseous.

In desperation I called Sylvia, then called a cab to take me to the local Hilton. I waited in the lobby for her to come. No questions asked, she drove 120 miles to rescue me, took me home to her bed, and let me cry. That's friendship. The next day Al was back on track and came for me. He took me to the doctor, who adjusted my medications, and I went home and stayed in bed for a week.

In turn, I've become a person my friends readily turn to for help or a sympathetic ear. Claudia says I can tune in to the underlying message, the plea for help or understanding, and people know I'm really listening. Jennifer says she can unburden herself to me because she knows I truly love her. I give my honest opinion, she says, and that's why people lean on me for support. "You tell it like it is."

I recently accompanied a friend to a weekend retreat to help her cope with her mother's death. She was worried that she had lost her faith, riddled with guilt that she'd felt only relief when her mother died. No one could convince her that her mother's death, after a two-year battle with brain cancer, was a blessing. She needed time to think, to hibernate, but she was feeling fragile, so I went along for emotional support. After three days of lectures, yoga, and pastoral serenity, my friend was still confused, weepy, and dismayed. On the third day, she gave up trying to unravel her emotions and we went to the movies. I was afraid I'd failed her. But when she returned home, my friend reported to her husband, "In the middle of the movie I realized that I just needed a friend."

My outlook has changed so much in recent years that it is hard for me to identify with the woman I now write about. The negative, self-centered Lisa Fittipaldi, who needed constant validation, who bridled at every remark, who rejected well-meant concern, embarrasses me. But finally I have forgiven her. I have compassion for her self-righteousness and her deep pain. I have forgiven her for the four years she wasted in self-pity and denial. To quote Shakespeare's *The Tempest,* I am now "all dedicated to closeness and the bettering of my mind."

I was feeling the need to take some kind of direct action to make life better for the blind, to make up for my years of complaining. While I've never had a political agenda, I'd certainly been frustrated by the policies of some organizations that work with the blind. I was a big fan of the president of the National Federation of the Blind, Kenneth Jernigan. Blind from birth, he lived a full and adventurous life, somehow managing to navigate the world without a cane. I'm so envious. He railed against the labeling and infantilizing of the blind. Jernigan had been a primary inspiration to me in my decision to find alternative strategies to sight that enable me to live in the world.

It irked me that some nonprofits that serve the blind seemed to pander to the public's view of the poor, helpless blind, drumming up sympathy in order to raise money. Of course, many organizations are limited in funding and strapped for personnel. Others are mired in pre–technology rehabilitation modalities, and fail to promote the tremendous advances in computer technology for the blind. I understand that each organization has its own niche, and helps in a particular way.

But given my experience and temperament, I lean toward organizations that are proactive in helping the blind maximize their independence, especially by taking advantage of technological advances. These include mobile communication devices, orientation and mobility guides, audio descriptive technologies, talking calculators and watches, speech-recognition software, Braille translation software, and numerous adaptive computer devices. A program called JAWS reads to me as I surf the Web or check my e-mail. Editing functions allow me to skim and skip around. As I write this book, JAWS scrolls back and forth at my voice commands. Braille was too slow and cumbersome for me. And what good does it do me? *Is there Braille on my cereal box? My mail? On labels in the stores?* Ironically, my failing hearing is forcing me to improve my Braille skills because it may turn out to be my only means of communicating with the world.

In 1999, with funding from the Lions Clubs of Carrollton and Georgetown, Texas, I started the Mind's Eye Foundation. The foundation acts as a clearinghouse for public awareness about blindness. The main goal of this nonprofit charity is to provide adaptive computers, scanners, and screen-reading software for blind, visually impaired, and hearing-impaired schoolchildren. This technology enables these children to remain mainstreamed in public schools and learn on a par with their sighted peers. The foundation's Web site, www.mindseyefoundation.com, is underwritten by several of our patrons.

During this period I set myself the difficult task of integrating multiple figures in complex backgrounds. The lone figure doesn't seem to interest me anymore. Recently, Nora was showing a painting of mine of a solitary French bicyclist to a friend. "Have you ever noticed that Lisa rarely paints a single figure?" her friend remarked. I was taken aback, but I had to admit that she was right. This simple remark helped me understand why I'm so afraid of losing my hearing. The auditory aspects of motion, crowds, and action, not the static figure, spark my internal visions. As my health declines, the scenes, characters, and action of my inner visualizations are getting more complex, perhaps as a way to fill the sensory void. The more challenging the task, the happier I am standing at the canvas. My goal is to someday paint a thousand people bathing on the banks of the Ganges River.

One of the by-products of my new fame—and my desire to raise money for the Mind's Eye Foundation—is that I am frequently invited to speak to civic and social organizations. My hosts usually specify the topic and tell me a bit about their activities, permitting me to tailor my remarks to their members. Usually I speak about blindness, art, and life in some combination. An interesting phenomenon occurs when I give a talk or an interview. Since I can't see my audience or any television cameras and I don't have to move around, I'm not at all self-conscious. Usually I just perch atop a platform or desk with my legs curled up under me as I speak, attuned to the audience's restlessness and anticipating the questions of the interviewer.

I often find that the audience expects some kind of inspirational tale, but I have a hard time coming up with something uplifting or encouraging to say. There's no way to sugarcoat the hard truth that blindness is truly awful, and living with a chronic disease requires endurance. If I've learned anything, I tell them, it's that there's no viable alternative but to make the best of any bad situation. The crucial thing I've discovered about living with a chronic illness is that you have to live. You have to untangle yourself from the knots of the past and the ineffective energies of the present. Remind yourself that you own your body. A healthy emotional relationship with your body is possible even though it is no longer young, healthy, and perfect. The secret passwords are *adaptation* and *change*. I am still learning this lesson. I can usually have my audience in stitches with tales of my avoidance, whining, and sheer orneriness. But I also talk about some of the hard-won lessons—and thus the hard-won contentment—of my current life.

Having run the gamut of emotional responses, I've developed specific strategies that help me cope with my chronic disease. At the core of all these strategies are attention and perseverance. The energy I once spent on anger and denial I now apply just as doggedly to making every detail of my life more positive and productive.

Anyone who has rehabbed themselves from alcohol or drugs will tell you that every day brings a new challenge that must be faced head-on. Anyone who has managed to extract themselves from an abusive relationship will tell you that the hard part is *staying* away. The first three days of a diet are easy. The third week is rough, when you're again having trouble zipping your pants. You have to stay the course. You accept the fact that there is no easy way out, no way of doing an end run around your problems. Change happens whether or not you actively choose it. You'll save yourself a lot of heartache if you choose it, and if you exercise some control over the direction it takes.

Midshipmen's Ball, 1974

Our first formal affair as newlyweds. Al was an officer in the United States Navy and this was his first formal event.

After-Race Party, 1989

We volunteered in flagging and communication at SCCA and CART automobile track events. This was in Detroit after a big win for our favorite team.

Twenty-fifth Wedding Anniversary, 1999

What a surprise! Our friends gave us this party to commemorate our first twenty-five years of marriage.

Working in My Studio, 2004

Here I'm working in my studio on the painting *An Eye for an Eye* and other works in progress. I like to work on a variety of paintings at one time, and they are usually in different states of completion.

Lisa, Al, and Wizard, 2003
Outside on the patio of our home in San Antonio, Texas.

The Beauregard House, 2004
The front-door view of Beauregard House, our bed-and-breakfast in San Antonio, Texas. Often you'll find me making muffins in the kitchen or talking with the guests.

JARS

Watercolor on paper 1995 11" × 30" Collection of the artist

Painted with a child's watercolor set on hot-press watercolor paper, *Jars* was my angry, frustrated response to Al's challenge that I do something constructive in response to losing my vision. The simple act of painting *Jars* was a turning point that eventually led to my career as an artist. In essence, it is the illusion of color as seen by the mind's eye.

DOUG'S BIRTHDAY

Watercolor on paper 1995 22" × 30" Private collection

I painted this canvas in Ruston, Louisiana, as a tribute to my instructor, M. Douglas Walton, for his birthday. This watercolor on paper utilizes tertiary colors to provide a variety of vibrant grays, a technique that I used when I was teaching myself to draw and paint. It was awarded first place for abstract art at my first statewide juried exhibition.

CALIFORNIA BANTAMS

Watercolor on paper 1995 22" × 30" Private collection

For several reasons, *California Bantams* has a special place in my heart. It is the first painting I sold at my first outdoor professional show. It is the first in a series of whimsical pieces. And it is the first of many impressionistic pieces I produced in watercolor from 1995 to 1998.

TROPICAL TIGER

Watercolor on paper 1996 22" × 30" Collection of the artist

Faced with the challenge "You will never be an artist because you can't paint animals,"
I obsessively proceeded to paint as many animals as I could, everything from cows to fish to
zebras and tigers. To lend him dignity, I painted the toothless old tiger in a field of orchids.

BEST BIKE RACE EVER:
THE WINNER

Watercolor on paper 1997
20" × 30"
Private collection

This is a double-page
illustration for a chil-
dren's book. The blank
area on the upper left
was left open for the
text. The plates for the
project were
completed, but the
book was never
published.

SUNSHINE SISTERS

Watercolor on paper 1997 22" × 15" Collection of Nick Lees

While exhibiting at an outdoor street show in Florida, I happened across these two women who called themselves the Sunshine Sisters. They volunteered their time as clowns to entertain children and the elderly at local hospitals. I was so taken by their caring nature and their willingness to share their joy in life that I was compelled to capture their zest in this watercolor.

TELLER OF TALES

Watercolor on paper 1999
22" × 30"
Collection of Jonathan Pikoff

I painted this canvas when I returned from my first visit to Mexico. Walking through a churchyard in Taxco with friends, I overheard three old men telling tales about their youth. From these snippets of conversation came the idea for this painting, the second in a series of public park-bench scenes.

JUST FOR KICKS

Mixed media on canvas 2002 36" × 48" Collection of the artist

This trio of dancers was painted as a demonstration piece for the Golden Paint Company. Their faces are done in oils, and their costumes in acrylics. *Just for Kicks* is part of a series of mixed-media paintings on canvas that explores dance and the possibilities of movement. I often return to the challenge of painting ballet, flamenco, ballroom, and jazz dance themes, especially fully detailed figures on a spare background.

OLÉ

Oil on canvas 2002 36" × 24" Collection of Marion Serelis

Painted in oil for *People* magazine, *Olé* appeared on the cover of a pharmaceutical journal in 2003. Emotion and feeling can be captured through movement and expression of the body. In this instance, I found the back and upper torso to be as dynamic as the front of the human body.

WHITBY

Oil on canvas 2003 48" × 36" Collection of Johnette Venne

Meandering along the English coastline in 2002, Al and I happened upon the quaint seaside village of Whitby. To paint the water reflected on the rain-slick streets, I had to call on everything that I had taught myself over the past seven years. Painting the diverse architecture, the signage on the buildings, the flags, the rain, and people huddled under umbrellas reassured me that I had made great strides in handling complex compositions with accuracy, precision, color balance, and linear perspective.

AFTER MIDNIGHT

Oil on canvas 2003 36" × 24" Collection of Jason and Christina Wagner

This allegorical painting depicts a woman whose party is over. Although she is tired, she is more dispirited that she is all dressed up with no place to go. This painting appears in the Revolution Studios movie *Cheer Up,* with Tommy Lee Jones.

THE BALLERINA

Oil on canvas 2003 40" × 30" Collection of Natalie Maines

I'm a big fan of Degas and share his love of movement and dance. This painting gives the viewer a glimpse into the professional dancer's life of toil and dedication. This painting taught me the techniques for painting soft light and the profile.

December in Paris

Oil on canvas 2003 40" × 30" Collection of Jim and Kelly Luedeke

Many times—both before and after losing my sight—Al and I strolled along the Left Bank in Paris, breathing in the fragrance of the flowers offered by the vendors in the markets of the Latin Quarter. I originally painted this piece in watercolor. But several years later I painted this version in oils, to resolve my uncertainty about my ability to re-create something I had previously painted.

L&M Café

Oil on canvas 2003
30" × 40"
Collection of Sandy and
Jim Evans

The L&M Café in Georgetown, Texas, was a breakfast hangout where a diverse assembly of local farmers, railroad engineers, and local college professors discussed daily events and politics over strong cups of coffee.

SHOW JUMPER

Oil on canvas 2003 40" × 30" Courtesy of Gallery Soco

I find the musculature of the horse as challenging to paint as the complexities of the human form. Large and formidably powerful animals, horses are yet able to move with grace and beauty. This painting strengthened my confidence that I could alter the perspective and retain an integral design.

FIGS

Oil on canvas 2003
16" × 20"
Collection of Mirtille Romegialli

My intention with *Figs* was to paint a unified tonal piece while creating shape and form within an impressionistic field. The only still-life painting of fruit that I have ever done, it was created in response to a visit to the Rijksmuseum in Amsterdam.

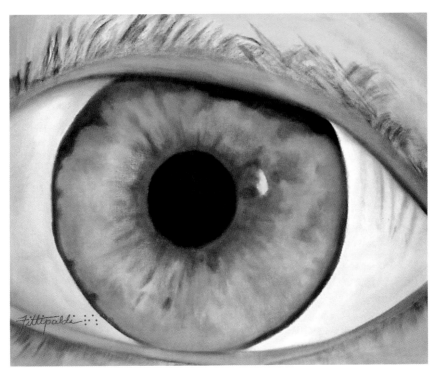

AN EYE FOR AN EYE

Oil on canvas 2004 16" × 20" Courtesy of Gallery Soco

Several critics have remarked that there must be some psychological reason that I do not paint eyes on my characters. Eyes, after all, are considered the windows to the soul. So I painted this piece.

Portobello Road

Oil on canvas 2004 48" × 36" Courtesy of Gallery Soco

During a recent visit to London, I was enthralled with the vendors and shops along Portobello Road. This painting was designed so that the various planes and perspectives create an illusion of imbalance; the painting always appears to be hanging at an angle. Although the foreground images predominate, the focal point is the smaller figure to the rear of the painting.

One needs a tremendous store of energy, organization, attention, and intellectual focus to live a full life as a blind person with a chronic disease. I am always multitasking, because even simple procedures are complex when the lights are off. I must analyze and synthesize gobs of information just to get from one end of the room to another. The more independence I desire, the harder I have to work. It's exhausting.

Fatigue rules my life. I have to be very careful not to get overtired, or my vasculitis symptoms will kick up. I ask myself maintenance questions. "Do you need a nap?" "Have you taken your medicine?" "What would give you energy now?" "Should you be doing this?" I conserve my energy, eliminating all nonessentials. Some days I just sit in my studio and ponder my next move. Maybe I sharpen a pencil or listen to an art lecture on tape. Some days I don't get out of bed at all. Other days I am a whirlwind of activity. I'll paint for eighteen hours straight, bake a week's supply of muffins, or go out for a movie marathon with my girlfriends.

There was a time when I consumed self-help books, looking for answers to my problems. But most of them are written by people who are watching from the bleachers—the therapists and health-care professionals. Even the first-person stories rarely spoke to me. Not that I didn't pick up some great tips from self-help books, but I came to the conclusion that coping is personal, individual. Some of us do it best with an audience, while others escape to a quiet beach with a book. I am married to someone who listens to me. I transform my woes into happier scenes on canvas. I have coffee with a friend or zone out with music. I still tend to keep my own counsel, but I no longer hesitate to call a friend. Sometimes it helps to write about whatever is bothering me, then crumple up the paper and throw it away. I learned that from a self-help book.

I rely on lists to keep myself on track. Al teases me about my compulsive list-making, but it works. I keep a running agenda of things to do. Mostly these are small tasks, like returning a phone call, getting in touch with a friend I haven't spoken to for months, answering some of the Mind's Eye e-mails, or paying the bills. I have Al read me the list every day, then I follow through and won't cross anything off until it's handled. Because I no longer have the luxury of letting tasks mount up or letting my life get out of order, I have finally broken my life-long habit of procrastinating.

I've set high standards for the way I interact with others. Now that I've learned tolerance, my world includes people from all walks of life. Niki says that because I can't see people, I'm not prejudiced by appearances. It's great not to think about or care what people look like, what they wear. A strange thing happens as your visual memory fades. Attuned to voices, scent, and energetic clues, you forget that the people you encounter even have these qualities, that they wear certain clothes or look a certain way.

Self-image acts as a blueprint for behavior. I've come to believe that in order to change the way you behave, you must change the way you think. You have to decide who you are and act accordingly. I put a smile on my face and in my voice. I use positive adjectives to describe myself. If I describe myself as patient and happy, I feel that way, and I treat others with patience and happiness. It took me a long time to get over my lifelong wariness of others' motives, to learn to be generous and thankful for all the help and support I receive.

Every Sunday I make a list of bad habits that showed up in the prior week. These might include believing that the glass is half empty, eating food that will provoke hives or asthma, not getting enough exercise, not calling to check in with my brother, forgetting to walk Wizard, not rescuing a friend in need, and interrupting people when they're talking. Every time I have a negative thought or do something negative, I immediately substitute a positive thought or action. When I have trouble learning some task, such as using the new toaster oven, I force myself to do it over and over until I can handle it, and I don't chastise myself for not doing it right.

I never put more than ten things on my "bad girl" list at once, and I try to eliminate one each week. For example, when I paid close attention to my habit of interrupting, I managed to shake it within a few weeks. The one about the glass being half empty tagged along for years, but I've finally been able to cross it off my list.

I keep my word, which increases my self-confidence and is an organizing factor in my life. I say no to things I don't want to do or don't have the energy to complete. I've trained myself to express what I need in a clear and forceful manner, without offending others. I have learned how to get attention in a store, to be helped down the stairs, to get someone to usher me to a seat in the movie theater. I smile a lot, and actually find joy in tackling my frustrations.

Eliminating bad habits, I've found, is good for my spirit. I feel like a better person, a better friend and helpmate. I no longer get in a stew over petty annoyances. I don't get upset if I spill paint and have to spend an hour cleaning up the mess. The person in front of me in the grocery line who can't find her checkbook and is scrabbling for coins in the bottom of her purse is no longer an annoyance; she entertains me. I can enjoy the drama of this once upsetting event. I'm more optimistic. I trust myself.

Whatever I accomplish, I make a point of patting myself on the back. "Good girl, Lisa," I tell myself, "you put away your brushes." "Good girl, you didn't interrupt," I say, or "That was great, you primed that canvas today." Most of us don't give ourselves enough credit for getting through a day.

Whenever I speak, the conversation eventually turns to my painting. The audience always wants to know how it is possible to paint without sight. How can you paint people if you can't see them? Why do so many of your pictures depict foreign scenes? How do you keep track of the lines on the canvas? How do you achieve a feeling of depth and distance? I will usually go off on a tangent about whatever interests me at the moment—perspective, color balance, focus, spatial management. I remember spending half an hour carrying on about mental mapping to a rapt audience of Rotarians in Cleveland.

Everyone, I pointed out, has some way of storing memories of the places they've been—their childhood home, their present workplace, the layout of the main street of their town, the order of their desk drawers or closets. A mental map is a selective representation of reality, and is dependent on how an individual person thinks. Each of you, I said, if asked to draw a map of the street outside this meeting hall, would do it differently. Some of you would be able to reproduce the scene in great detail, in three dimensions. Others would barely recall what was there and could not proceed without looking out the window. Others would come up with only the sketchiest layout, and the proportions would be skewed. Each of you would give importance to different factors—the trees, the local bar, the street numbers. To some of you, color would be important, to others proportion or distances. If you want to check out your information, you need only step outside.

For a blind person, having a mental-mapping technique is critical, which is why I paint. Painting solidifies my memory bank. From what I understand, every blind person has a different way of mapping his or her world. Some blind people have such trouble with spatial issues that they never become comfortable venturing beyond their front door. I have read about others who have amazing visualization abilities. An article by Oliver Sacks in the July 24, 2003, *New Yorker* mentioned a few cases: a former carpenter who single-handedly replaced the roof guttering on his multigabled house; a blind biologist who identifies new species of mollusks by using his enhanced tactile ability to recognize minute variations in the shape and form of their shells.

My ace in the hole is a photographic memory. I code, store, and then decode information, using a geometric logic to define my environment. In a sense, I project information from diverse sources onto an internal screen that represents the piece of the world I am trying to replicate. My fading visual imagery is supplemented by new memories created through sound and touch. Years after the fact, I can recall a person by the conversations we have had. I remember events by their sounds. There is a kinetic aspect to memory as well. I remember events according to specific patterns of movement, both mine and the motions of my surroundings.

When I move around any environment, real or virtual, I build a detailed mental image that allows me to shift around in that space, whether it is a room or a canvas, whether it is a checkbook in which I write or a table on which I place a cup of tea. I must constantly edit the scene as new information is gathered, to keep up with any changes. There is a continual feedback loop between the environment and the internal visual display I create.

Speaking engagements involve traveling—mostly air travel. I love to travel, don't I? I'm always game for escape of any kind. But almost every time I travel alone I have an awful time of it and swear I'll never do it again. This vow lasts until the next time I'm invited to speak, when I find myself going back for more. In the face of all evidence to the contrary, I continue to delude myself into believing that I'm mobile enough to handle any situation and that the airlines will smoothly accommodate my needs. Somehow, I tell myself, this time it will all work out fine. Perhaps I still crave drama, and forget that it often comes at the expense of my equilibrium and sanity. Sometimes I think that the only upside of traveling to speaking engagements is that I can count on having an entertaining horror story with which to warm up the audience.

I have learned so much about myself from airports—good, bad, and truly sidesplitting. Here are a few air-travel tales to amuse and horrify you, beginning with the time Al dropped me at San Antonio International Airport for a flight to a speaking engagement in Atlanta. My usual excited anticipation of a new adventure turned to overwhelm the minute he drove away. Everything seemed darker than usual, and the surging swarms of travelers made it extra difficult to distinguish any stationary shapes. I called out for assistance, but without a guide dog to signal my condition, I was ignored. Airport Lesson No. 1: Not only am I blind, but I am invisible to others.

Finally some kind soul walked me to a ticket counter, but it must have been the wrong one, because the agent informed me that I needed to move on. But move on where? I was frozen in place. Getting no response, I broke into helpless, shoulder-shaking tears. Embarrassed as I was, I was laughing on the inside at my outburst. Here I am headed to Atlanta to talk to the Young Presidents Club about being strong in the face of adversity, about adaptation and change, about the ability to paint or some such notion. But I am sobbing at the ticket counter, holding up a line of impatient passengers, and not adapting at all. The harried agent called someone over to deal with the nutcase. The Kleenex box appeared, tears were dried, apologies were made, and I was escorted onto the plane.

At which point what I call the Flying Therapist Syndrome kicked in. I was settled into my seat, still snuffling a bit, when the man next to me leaned over to tell me that it must be terrible to be blind. This is another aspect of air travel that I manage to forget about between flights. People have no qualms about sharing their reactions. Typically they start out empathetic, progress swiftly to prodding questions about blindness, and conclude with their opinion that I should not be permitted to travel alone. I try to remember Al's admonition to think of myself as an "ambassador" for the blind, educating people about vision loss, demonstrating by example that blindness is not a death sentence. I'm no longer so insulted and defensive that I blatantly refuse to answer questions, but frequently the stress of travel makes me want to close my eyes and sleep on the plane. I have finally understood, however, that most people are genuinely interested in what I have to say, and that their sympathy is well intended. I even admit that at times others' perspectives offer me unexpected insight. Okay, the truth is that I am the constant beneficiary of others' help and concern.

I'm less keen on being a confessor for my fellow travelers. Almost without fail, after a few questions about my blindness, my companions will unburden themselves of their darkest secrets—the scary credit card debt, the alcoholic spouse, the time they stole money from the cash box, their eating disorder. I don't think it's because I'm such a sympathetic listener. I assume people confide in me because, like the priest in the confessional, I can't see them. Their secret is safe with me. Besides, I can't get up and leave.

I try my best to avoid travel mishaps, calling ahead to warn the airlines that I will need assistance. On rare, wonderful occasions, it all goes smoothly—an attendant is waiting at the end of the ramp, a cart is ready to take me to the next terminal, someone gets me seated and comfortable on the plane and sees that I'm met at the other end. It's a tremendous relief. But more often my advance planning is fruitless. When I am left stranded, my rescuers invariably ask why I didn't inform the ticket agent that I'd need help. So much for assertiveness.

When I decided to fly solo to speak in Toronto, I had to change planes twice, in Dallas and then at O'Hare. No problem. I was several years into blindness by this time, a pro! Help was prearranged between airports, but no one materialized. Finally an attendant showed up, pointed at something or other, and told me that she would meet me "over there" in a moment. Furious, I held up my cane and demanded that she describe exactly where I was to be, as I could not see where she was pointing. She got angry and walked off.

Now I was late for the plane change from Dallas to O'Hare, alone in the terminal trying to get someone to notice me. I had to make a decision. Shall I be a polite adult or a spoiled child? Which will get me where I need to go? I tried adult mode first. Whenever I heard a noise nearby I'd call out, "Can you help me?" It seemed no one could. Precious minutes ticked by, and my frustration mounted. I raised my voice and shouted, but I still received no assistance. Not until I started waving my cane in the air did people understand why I was making a spectacle of myself. Someone finally guided me to the designated spot, but the attendants were angry that I'd showed up late.

Because of my embarrassment in Dallas, I tried to negotiate the maze from the domestic terminal to the international terminal at O'Hare by myself. This maze walking did not go so well for me, and I rapidly became disoriented. So again I tried to ask directions. Hearing a motorized cart, I stepped into its path to get assistance. A man who never identified himself whisked me away. He was so upset that I was wandering the airport unassisted that he called the airline and attempted to get an attendant to aid me. After he was put on hold several times, he tried the gate desks, then the airline information desks. Finally he gave up and physically delivered me to a check-in counter and demanded that I be helped. When he did not get a quick enough response, he took me by the arm and escorted me to the international terminal and placed me in the care of the agent at the check-in counter. I was humiliated but thankful. It was comforting to know that at least one person could share my never-ending frustration.

Last year I flew from San Antonio to speak in Wichita, Kansas. It all started out very well. A hospitable attendant appeared as requested to meet me in Dallas and help me change planes. He asked me where I was going and at what time. I told him, and showed him my boarding pass. We proceeded down a hall on a motorized cart and onto an elevator, speeding along to Terminal A with just enough time to catch the shuttle flight. We boarded the tram and arrived at the gate, climbed the outside stairs to the plane, and I was ensconced in an aisle seat of a small turboprop. Out of curiosity, I asked the arrival time of the flight to Kansas. The shocked flight attendant informed me that the flight was going to Wichita Falls, Texas, and that I was obviously confused as to my destination. When I assured her that I was most definitely going to Kansas, she patted me on the head and said, "Sweetie, don't worry about it, you'll be just fine."

This was not the first time I'd been treated as though my mental faculties had disappeared because I was toting a cane. I began noisily badgering the attendants, who were concentrating on getting everyone seated and stowed. I was so annoying, fortunately, that they finally looked at my ticket and boarding pass. Sure enough, the crazy lady was supposed to be going to Wichita, Kansas. I was quickly rushed off the plane and plunked just outside the boarding gate. It was noon; in less than an hour I was scheduled to give a keynote address at a luncheon in Wichita. Instead, I was sitting at the wrong gate waiting for the irritated attendants to decide what to do with me. They kept asking me why I hadn't mentioned that I was going to Wichita. Now they had to find another attendant, repeat the transfer process from shuttle to tram to cart and rebook my flight. Convinced that it was my fault that I'd ended up on the wrong plane, they weren't nice about it. I had to change airlines, because by this time I had missed my scheduled flight. Miraculously, I arrived only an hour late.

As usual, I showed up with an amusing story (glossing over the scared, angry parts). I was tired and starving and desperately needed to find a ladies' room. But I was rushed into the luncheon to speak to a group of two hundred eager sorority women, feeling unprepared and rather discombobulated. They hadn't given me a topic, so I was particularly at sea. I prefer to have some idea of what the group wants to hear about. I flailed around, trying to pull together a coherent presentation, but I'm afraid I just blathered from one subject to another until they cleared the dessert plates. I felt as if I'd let them down, but a few weeks later a check for twenty-five hundred dollars arrived for the Mind's Eye Foundation. I finally learned my air-travel lesson, and now I accept speaking engagements only if Al can accompany me.

———————

In November 1999, I awoke in the middle of the night in the middle of a full-on panic attack. I knew for certain that I would never sell another painting, that my life as an artist was *over.* I strode out to my studio to pack away the brushes and paints and called Claudia. "I cannot continue trying to force my way into the art world," I whimpered. (Picture me in my jammies with my arm flung across my feverish brow.) "I need a job."

"Just what you need, more drama," she laughed. "It's four o'clock in the morning. Go back to bed." Some friend. I made my way downstairs to the office and began surfing the Internet. *Change. I need a change.* Finding and discarding one get-rich-quick scheme after another, I came across a Web site that listed bed-and-breakfast businesses for sale. *Perfect.* The ideal business for a couple. The ideal way to have a social life and get myself out of my suburban isolation. I scooted back to the bedroom and shook Al into wakefulness to announce that I'd found our new life.

Al did not want a new life. Al is a homebody, and our beautiful house in Georgetown was his nest. He was perfectly content. He loved the neighborhood and our house. He liked hanging out with his cronies at the coffee shop. He relished his roles as chauffeur, gardener, and cook. He hates cities and urban life. Having moved around so much during his navy years, he just wanted to stay put, cut his grass, and play golf.

I detested living in hard-core suburbia, where I felt like a prisoner in my own home. I was bored, bored, bored. I had been droning on about moving from Georgetown since return-ing from Ruston. I wanted to sell everything and travel. I wanted to get a job and live where I could take public trans-portation. *I just want to get on a bus.* I updated my résumé and began making preparations to move.

I was done grieving for my lost vision. I no longer painted to prove that the blind can do anything if given a chance. I no longer felt compelled to be the world's greatest painter. I no longer needed to be on a soapbox. For lack of outside stimuli, I was spending ten hours a day, seven days a week in my studio, trying to resolve technical problems and improve my skills. I mastered cast shadows and the musculature of horses. I prac-ticed painting hands and the intricate folds of clothing. I was keeping my mind occupied, keeping the dark monsters at bay. But without fresh material for inspiration, it was hard going. My mental filing cabinet was emptying fast. I craved texture, passion, variety. I needed juice. It was imperative that I return to real life, real people, and sounds and events.

Al dug in his heels. He could not understand why painting could not satisfy all my needs. I tried to explain that the art of painting had less to do with the dexterity of my hand than the ability to analyze with my mind, and my mind was stagnating. We had one of the few really serious arguments in our mar-riage. Neither of us wanted to budge.

We went around and around about moving for two months. "I have no choice on this issue," I pleaded. "If we don't move, I'll emotionally vanish." Remaining in our Austin commuter community was not something I was willing to compromise on, and I was packing for parts unknown. I started the new year threatening, "Either we move together or I move alone."

Al finally relented. "We can look," he conceded, "but I'm not promising anything." Scouring the Internet, I turned up several promising operations in Maryland, Virginia, and South Carolina. I sent away for information, talked with the brokers for these properties, and made plans for a road trip. I signed us up for an inn-management course in North Carolina. I started to clean the closets.

CHAPTER TEN

AN ARTIST WHO HAPPENS TO BE BLIND

The artist is a person who is expert in the training of perception.

—MARSHALL MCLUHAN

CLAUDIA WAS LESS THAN ENTHUSIASTIC about my new master plan. In the hope of heading off disaster, she suggested I visit an acquaintance who sold real estate in San Antonio. Once I understood that running a bed-and-breakfast was no picnic, she figured, I would return to sanity and painting. My physicians were against any move to a new environment, much less a return to work. Some felt that even painting was too strenuous for my precarious health.

Never mind. I was convinced that the change would be good for me, for Al, and for the state of our economic affairs. So we took a drive to San Antonio and met with Claudia's real estate agent acquaintance. To give us a taste of the bed-and-breakfast life, he took us to several operating properties. These inns weren't on the market, he explained, but we would have an opportunity to speak with the owners. When we remained unconvinced of the problems and labor involved, he drove us to a bed-and-breakfast in a turn-of-the-century Victorian in the historic King William district, owned by a friend who was at his wit's end trying to keep it afloat. The house was a horror in dire need of repair, a shining example of why we did not want the headaches of running an inn. As the agent described the condition of the house and enumerated the problems of running a bed-and-breakfast, I began to doubt that my judgment was sound. Everyone's concerns made sense. I was not up to the obligation or the work involved.

Al was. The minute we drove up the shady lane to the Beauregard House, Al wanted it. I panicked. *What was I think-ing?* I tripped twice before we even got to the front door, once on the broken brick of the walkway, and again on a rickety front step. How would I be able to learn my way around a new home? How was I going to be able to deal with the public? How would we manage, me with my blindness, Al with his unstable moods and short-term memory deficits? I cried and threatened and begged for us to stay in Georgetown. But Al loved the place. He also saw a good business opportunity, and he made an offer that persuaded the owner to sell. We plunked down our money and headed back to suburbia to pack our bags. For three months I could not sleep, fretting about the money and yes, the *change*.

On April Fools' Day 2000 we moved into the Beauregard House, paid for with the sale of my paintings. Calamity struck on the first night, in the form of a violent thunder and light-ning storm. Hail pounded the roof, rain poured in from dozens of leaks around the house. I couldn't find the kitchen, let alone a pot. But Al put my mind at ease. "Don't worry about finding a pot," he told me. "The roof leaks in too many places for any pot to make a difference."

I knew we were in trouble. Miss Fiscal Responsibility had not budgeted for major repairs, and Al had not accurately con-veyed the alarming condition of the wreck we'd purchased. Given the dilapidation of the house and the dire warnings of an insurance agent, Al soon decided he did not want the responsibility of running an inn.

No ghosts appeared, but I was scared. I had forgotten what it was like to be blind in an unfamiliar place. I'd lived in Georgetown for years before losing my sight, but I had no mental picture of my new surroundings. There were few cues to give me a sense of distance, space, and form. There were too many windows but too little light. Too many doors going off in every direction, multiple stairways, and long halls. Echoes everywhere made every room feel the same. I could not find the kitchen. I could not find my shoes. I needed assistance at every step. I was a stranger in a strange land—my new home.

The idiocy of our move was staggering. My new social worker was flabbergasted that we'd purchased a multistory house, as I was still clumsy on curbs, much less a whole flight of stairs. Since my foray to Ruston, I hadn't been upgrading my ability to navigate new territory. Which meant I'd not been paying attention to the fact that my vision level had fallen to virtually zero. I would never see my new home, and I could not fathom for the life of me why I'd wanted to move. Yes, the trolley stop was on the corner. But I was afraid to go as far as the bathroom alone; the prospect of taking a bus was frightening. For three weeks, I cried and cried and cried. But when my tears finally dried, I was still at the Beauregard House.

I called in the troops. Friends came to clear out piles of trash and broken furniture, making daily trips to the dump. They cleaned the windows and transoms. They disinfected and swept. They raked and caulked and painted. Al's friend Greg painted the downstairs rooms. Claudia wiped down the musty halls while she gave me moral support and encouragement. Niki unpacked dishes and organized the storage spaces. Raye lent his support by rewiring the house for television and telephones, while Sylvia

scrubbed down the kitchen. Everyone was appalled—appalled!—
that Al had purchased a house that resembled a slum and smelled
like soggy day-old bread. They could not believe that we'd
traded a compact one-story ranch for this huge white elephant. I
kept threatening to go live with my friends. By the end of a week,
everyone was exhausted, but the house still wasn't habitable. So
more friends came to paint, clean, and haul trash. The movers
arrived and unpacked our belongings. My pals helped me organize my closet, down to the smallest detail, and set up my computer space. We were home.

At this juncture Al and I reviewed our finances and realized
that our plan to take the house private was a pipe dream. The
house still needed a roof, a kitchen upgrade, a complete wiring
and plumbing overhaul, a dining room, new tile in the bathrooms, a deck renovation, more painting and window replace-
ments . . . the list went on and on. What could we do? To pay
for our folly, we applied for a certificate of occupancy and reac-
tivated the bed-and-breakfast license.

I had gotten my wish. We were living in the middle of a city
and I had a bed-and-breakfast. All I had to do was learn to
clean, and cook, and play hostess. I was an innkeeper now, a
businesswoman, not an artist. Of course, I would have to first
learn how to get from the kitchen to the bedroom.

The plan was that Al would do the maintenance, pay the bills,
and help with the housekeeping. I agreed to do the cooking and
baking. This plan lasted two days, since I still could not turn on
the gas burners without catching my sleeves on fire. The ancient
oven did not hold temperatures accurately, so my muffins
wavered between burnt and raw. We needed a Web site and an
800 number. We needed a business plan and an operations routine. I called Claudia. She stayed for a month, leading me on
daily navigation forays around my new home and neighborhood.

Through a process of trial and error it was determined that I would oversee the finances and Al would do the cooking. All we needed now was a guest.

A taxi dropped off our first guests at the end of June, two women from Chicago who had flown to San Antonio on a whim to see Tina Turner in concert, unaware that it was a convention weekend and all the major hotels and inns in town were full. The cab driver, remembering that the Beauregard House had once been a bed-and-breakfast, dropped them on our doorstep. We had only one room completely done: our bedroom. Al and I knew nothing about running an inn, and we had no idea how to play host. But we offered our room to these two wayward souls to give the innkeeping business a whirl; we slept on the office floor.

From these guests came two others, and from them two more. By the end of August we had three more rooms painted, furnished, and decorated. The plumbers and electricians finally finished their work, and Wizard and I learned to navigate the stairs like old pros. Guests arrived and filled the rooms. We still thank Tina Turner for bringing us our first guests.

At some point between the sale of the house in Georgetown and our purchase of the Beauregard House in San Antonio I was offered a one-woman show in Miami at the Bal Harbour Gallery. I had not painted since the prior December and did not have enough paintings to open a show. The Beauregard House had no studio space, and my supplies and studio gear were in storage. In moving to San Antonio I had elected to give up painting. I was tired of the emotional upheaval; I could not seem to separate the art from the artist, or the individual from the disease. As the fates would have it, my new neighbor Ralph Medina remembered my work from an outdoor fair in San Antonio. Urging me to get back to painting, he offered me a trashed-out apartment for one hundred dollars a month to use as studio space.

I couldn't resist. Those creative ideas were flowing again, and it wasn't just because of the Bal Harbour show offer. I was finally getting the message. Being an artist concerned with creativity and self-expression and being a blind person who could paint were two different things. And I was an artist, it seemed. I would have to commit my life to hard work, experimentation, and improvement. I would have to learn to ignore the skeptical media and just paint. It was not something that could be extinguished with a change of location or a redirection of focus.

Our guests at the Beauregard House were a powerful influence in getting me back in the studio, not only because they loved (and bought) the paintings that hung on the walls, but because I became genuinely interested in them, their lives and stories, their texture and diversity. I hadn't given a hoot about people when I could see. They were just bodies to me, with assigned functions—movie buddy, lunch companion, shopping date. Now they are my lifeblood. There are constantly people around, and I love it. Today I don't cultivate people just because I can't see and need help, but because they are essential to my emotional well-being.

All I have to do is sit still and listen as our guests recount their adventures in San Antonio, their day on the golf course, or the weight-loss infomercial they watched on TV, and I have a story for a painting. The nuances of disposition and character, my interactions with guests as both voyeur and participant, the imagery triggered by conversations and the slice of life we share, all of these I try to bring to the canvas.

Even though I know it's silly, I still pride myself on appearing normal. I can't help it. We've had guests who didn't realize

I was blind until they'd been here for three days. I'll talk to them at breakfast, or I'll clear the table. They'll see me run across the courtyard to answer the phone. But later they're puzzled. "What's with Lisa?" they ask Al. "We waved to her when we came in this afternoon and she completely ignored us." So my cover is blown.

The guests at our table motivate me to explore new themes every time I stand at my easel. The energy of each group inspires a unique concept for a painting, with a specific color palette and a distinctive face for each person portrayed. Given my limitations, this leads to much frustration and countless failures. I want my paintings to be snapshots, still frames capturing a fleeting image, the refraction of light at a given moment. But this is impossible. The eye captures the still frame, and my eyes don't function. I must bypass the most crucial aspect of the relationship between the painter and his subject, which is visual observation. I can only depict an imaginary dialogue between the viewer and the artist, telling a version of the story based on my alternative means of picturing the scene. When I complete a painting, I always feel that I could have done it better, "if only" I had listened more closely. I cannot attempt a portrait likeness. I will always be on the outside of the scene, as a narrator is to the play, commenting but not participating, viewing the subjects from my unique turn of mind and from a position distant from reality.

The imagery for a particular painting doesn't always spring to mind full-blown. In some cases it builds up over time, an accumulation of inputs from several sources. A few years ago, Sylvia and I took a road trip to New Orleans. I was so overstimulated by the funeral processions in the streets, the Bourbon Street dives, the noises in the courtyards, the chaos of the waterfront, the hawkers and fortune-tellers, that I could not focus. The second day, in the Latin Quarter, Sylvia invited me to wander around and explore on my own. She patiently sat in a nearby café for nearly three hours, keeping an eye out for my safety, while I navigated the main square, listening, approaching people. I was enraptured with the rich tapestry of sound. No images came to me at the time, just a sense of energy. A group of street musicians tuned their instruments, improvising and getting ready for a formal jazz concert in the square. When they stopped playing, someone asked if I was lost. "Nope," I replied. "Just trying to figure out what you look like."

Four months later, I went to speak in Memphis, another city with its own distinctive flavor. When I returned, Sylvia called to plan a trip to the mall. We were reminiscing about Louisiana when a full-blown image of the New Orleans musicians appeared—a trio of jazz players in crisp white shirts against a dark, vine-covered wrought-iron fence. This mental imagery and the trip to Memphis coalesced in the painting *Beale Street Blues*. The point I am trying to make is that my experiences do not convert directly into a painting but are stored, combined, and then dusted off to be used later. Observations collected from sounds, conversations, and sense memories get stacked up in my internal filing cabinet like wafery sheets of onion-skin paper, to be delicately removed and overlaid for future use.

Movies are an excellent source of imagery. If the dialogue supports the movie, the imagery will follow. When the dialogue does not convey a sense of drama, suspense, action, or romance, no imagery arises. I love *The Lord of the Rings*, for example, because the allegory creates strong images of the characters. Sam, Gandalf, and the Dwarf spring to mind effortlessly. No one had to describe them to me. On several occasions I have drawn movie characters that people recognize. It's funny how the imagination lets you fill in the blanks. Passion, energy, and movement are essential to good visual imagery.

When crustiness, eccentricity, compassion, wit, or wisdom come through, in a character or person, I can paint them.

A newlywed couple who stayed with us last year recently returned to celebrate their anniversary. During our long talks on their first visit, I was taken with both of them and found them delightful. This time around, the four couples at the breakfast table were commenting on a painting called *Study for West Side Story* when the man on my left said to the newlyweds, "If we did not know better"—i.e., this being your first time here, Lisa being blind—"we would have assumed Lisa had used you for the models in that painting." I thought the comment was a little weird. Then someone remarked that the woman in the painting looked like she could be our guest's twin. The returning couple told me later that they were pleased that I had painted them into the study. I was perplexed to find that I had, apparently, convincingly conveyed their physicality from the kinds of clues I'm able to pick up. Everyone at the table had recognized them!

Seeing how I live and work, our guests often confide in me. "How come you're happy and I'm not happy?" they ask.

I, in turn, ask them why they're not happy and what they would like to do to change their situation. "What are you waiting for?" I ask. "What could you do right now?" A healthy and wealthy Boston woman who was here recently was distraught because now that her children were grown, she felt that her life served no purpose. Without the role of mother, she was lost. I asked her what would give her a sense of identity, and you know what she said? She told me that she would like to wear jeans like me. She went on to tell me about the years she'd competed on the beauty-pageant circuit—as had her daughters. She was well aware that she had accepted the circumscribed set of values and expectations of her world, but now she was chafing under its restrictions.

"Well, your husband has gone off golfing," I observed. "Why don't you go downtown to Dillard's and buy yourself a pair of jeans?" It seemed like a small thing, but it took her two days to work up the nerve to purchase the jeans, and another day to wear them to breakfast and show her husband. "You look great" was his comment. "Now I can go buy myself a pair of jeans."

Which led to a long discussion at the breakfast table about self-image and identity, about why it was so traumatic to buy that pair of jeans. If the jeans were a symbol of her coming into her own, I asked her, what did she want to do next?

"I want to sell my house," she replied. Her husband nearly choked on his strawberry soufflé. She's upped the ante. Here was a woman walking around inside a fifty-six-hundred-square-foot cube that someone else had built for her, and until recently she'd never questioned whether it was what she wanted.

"You don't have to create your own cube from scratch," I told her, "but you have to put what you need inside it, and arrange it to your liking." Having gone through a similar pattern of conformity in my own life before blindness, I understood how she felt. Today I know a good deal about creating an authentic life and not letting someone else do it for you. But I had to go blind and be forced, kicking and screaming, to change. Maybe she'll do it less traumatically. Perhaps, for starters, she won't have to sell her home.

In May 2000, the Bal Harbour Gallery in Miami sold sixteen major paintings on opening night. The gentleman who owns the gallery was so annoyed that I was fifteen minutes late for the opening that he barely acknowledged my presence. The fact that I'd been robbed by the cab driver on my way to the show and was distressed about having lost my identification and money was of no concern to him. I was taken aback by his rudeness, but the new me, who could handle all life threw at her, quickly calmed down and enjoyed the evening immensely.

The Bal Harbour show led to more gallery shows and more exposure and publicity. Next I had exhibitions at the Dallas Museum of Art and my friend Jason Siegel's new Gallery SOCO in Austin. After a gala opening at the Witte Museum in July 2001, cosponsored by the Lighthouse for the Blind and Red McCombs, my traveling show, Blind Ambition, made the first of eight stops at museums around the country. This retrospective covered the transition from my years painting in watercolor to my present oil paintings. An interactive display that accompanied the exhibit offered insights into vision loss as it relates to technology, art, creativity, and color.

The press loved my story. Each exhibit in a new area generated another round of press and television appearances. Al and I got used to being local celebrities, used to having our privacy invaded. It was our job and our livelihood. The Blind Ambition show was so successful that Al designed and built another custom-tailored studio for me. Our friends often comment on Al's great taste and color sense. I wouldn't know, but the space works wonderfully for me. He also designed and launched two more linked Web sites, www.beauregardhouse.com and, for those who know me by reputation if not by name, www.blindartist.com.

I had one last challenge to my determination go my own way as an artist. In May 2000 I received an e-mail from Michael O' Mahoney, owner of the Wentworth Gallery, with branches in Miami and Atlanta. He had seen my paintings at the Bal Harbour Gallery in Miami and wanted to sign me to an exclusive two-year contract. Even though I was making decent money selling my paintings through my Internet sites and periodic shows, I felt that I needed the financial stability and credibility that a major gallery would provide. And since I was still uncertain about whether my art was any good, an offer from the prestigious Wentworth seemed like validation.

There were a few stipulations. He insisted that I work in oils, because that's what collectors desired. I was to deliver two paintings a month, thirty-by-forty-inch canvases for which he would pay me five hundred dollars each. You'd think I would have learned my lesson after the disasters of the *Today* show and the illustration job. Hadn't I made a commitment to paint for myself only? But I was drawn to the idea of having a major gallery system to market my work, and the Wentworth is one of the country's largest. I signed the contract. It is a measure of my insecurity and my fervent desire to make it as an artist that I agreed to everything. Oh good, I reasoned, two paintings a month. *Finally I have a steady job.*

Jason encouraged me to try this new adventure. "You can afford to take the risk," he said. "Look at the contract as a way of being paid to take a crash course in oils." That turned out to be an understatement. In my rush to be represented by the Wentworth, I hadn't stopped to analyze what I was getting into. I didn't own oil paints, brushes, or canvas, and I had conveniently downplayed the fact that the toxicity of oil paints and mediums was terrible for my vasculitis. But hey, I wanted to play in the major leagues. I dropped watercolors and buried myself in the studio in a fevered quest to master oil painting and turn out the two paintings a month my contract stipulated.

I soon confirmed firsthand that oil and water don't mix. The technical aspects of watercolor and oil painting are almost diametric opposites. I was right back on that stool in Ruston, Louisiana, overwhelmed at having to master another new world.

I systematically studied the intricacies of hue and saturation, glazing and layered color, all the while trying to paint a recognizable form. Oil paints, with their long drying time and general messiness, are hard enough for the sighted painter to master. I sometimes felt as if I was trying to wade through mud to find light. The pigments and color system for working in oils differ markedly from those for watercolor. With watercolor, there is a textural boundary to the forms you are working with and a concrete method for determining space, orientation, and outcome. It's comparable to Braille; you can feel your way around. Working with the indeterminate boundaries of oil painting, I have no way of assessing what I have accomplished, what I have obliterated or enhanced. I operate, truly, on blind faith.

Painting twelve hours a day, seven days a week for a year was not enough for a crash course in oils. Between my energy limitations and the toxic fumes, the pressure of producing the two paintings a month was pushing me to the point of exhaustion. To meet my obligations, I was sending off paintings that were not up to my perfectionist standards. The first year, I felt that only four of the paintings were finished and acceptable. Although the gallery was selling my paintings at a huge markup, Al had to badger the staff every month for my paltry fees. For all that I was enjoying my new adventure with oils, my level of misery with the Wentworth was sapping my strength and spirit.

When my contract came up for review at the end of the year, I tried to renegotiate—to reduce the obligatory number of paintings, to raise my fees beyond the built-in 15 percent increase, and to have some flexibility regarding canvas size. The answers were no, no, and no. I decided that, for the sake of my health and sanity, I needed to get out of the contract.

Some financial analyst I was. I'd been so eager to be represented by the Wentworth that I had neglected to have an attorney review the contract. It turned out that, for a lousy five hundred dollars each, the Wentworth now owned the copyright to these paintings. I hired an attorney to help me break the contract, but it wasn't pretty. The gallery sent me a scathing letter saying that I didn't have the talent or purchasing power to demand more money or changes in the contract, implying that I'd never sell another painting. But I prevailed, and was soon free of my servitude to the Wentworth Gallery.

The Wentworth experience had taken a heavy toll, both the toxic mediums and the toxic relationship. My heart was weaker, and I was having intense flare-ups of vasculitis. A month after breaking the contract, I began a course of chemotherapy. Because it's an immune system depressant, chemotherapy, in carefully administered doses, is prescribed for advanced cases of vasculitis and other mediated immunological disorders. My head-in-the-sand attitude toward my health was not working. I needed to pay closer attention to the complex issues of coping with a chronic disease.

A chronic illness is one that persists over time without a definable beginning, middle, or end. Chronic disease is not a detour or a destination. It is a fact of life, part of who you are. I no longer think of my vasculitis as a crisis. It's just one more thing that defines me—I'm blind, I have green eyes, I'm married, I'm a painter, and I have vasculitis, with all its associated pain and restrictions.

A chronic disease does not go away. It is not amenable to a quick fix, and it cannot be ignored. You can only reframe your attitude about it. Adaptation, minute by minute, is the key to living with any chronic condition. Everyone has a horror of being incapacitated, of being disfigured or disabled. A recent guest confided that he was having ocular migraines, with the zigzag aura that often precedes their onset. But he refused to take a minimal dose of Norvasc for fear of appearing weak. Another guest pulled me aside to ask me how I live with an incurable disease. She is recovering from cancer and dreads its return. It seems that what people really fear is the unknown. Change, in the abstract, is frightening. What I try to tell them is that the suffering can be cured or abated, but not the illness itself. I compare integrating blindness to the Buddhist parable of the Warrior and the Dragon. You are the warrior, and since you can't slay the mighty dragon, you learn to wear asbestos so you don't burn to death.

Chronic diseases do not respect socioeconomic, religious, or racial lines. If you are lucky, you will make it to your seventies or eighties before you have a brush with cancer, diabetes, heart disease, stroke, or hearing or vision loss. But if you live long enough, you will inevitably have to contend with some form of chronic disease.

Vasculitis, like most chronic conditions, is a dictator. It is always emotionally or physically present, like the Microsoft operating system of my computer. I've come to think of it as the old bathrobe that can't be tossed out, the garage I will never clean. I am like the navigator of a ship that has only so much fuel to make it to shore. I am thrown by the tides of shifting emotions, tossed by waves of physical upheavals. Continual course correction is imperative. As Al says to me, "Just tell me what you are thinking and what you need." In other words, identify what is stressing me and what I can do about it. If there is nothing I can do about an issue, I let it go.

Stress management is the key. In the early stages of a chronic disease, stress is unavoidable. Even denial has its place. You cannot take in all that is happening to you at once or you will go under from the shock. In the early stages, you have to pace your ability to come to terms with your condition, and denial helps, up to a point. You slowly learn the parameters of your condition and formulate a plan to coexist with it. But stress is a perception, not an event. It needs to be acknowledged and managed. You have to find a way to be pleased in the moment, and to avoid prolonged, counterproductive grieving for the past or fretting about the future. You reach a milestone when you accept that control is an illusion. I had to learn to drop the unconscious behavioral traps—"I should have, I would have, I could have"—before I could accept my condition and its inconveniences.

Attitude counts. Changing the way you think changes the pattern of your life. Attitude adjustment is like dieting for the mind and spirit. Emotional eating sabotages the well-intentioned efforts of dieters, resulting in unwanted pounds, fatigue, and feelings of being undesirable and weak. When I am stressed I paint, sketch, or at least sit in the big armchair in my studio and think. I do yoga, listen to a favorite tape, meditate, or take Wizard for a walk around the block. Sometimes a deep breath or a moment of silence makes all the difference. It's the seconds of white space that we give ourselves that help us clock enough minutes to make a rational, beneficial response. I have learned to say to myself that the problem is never a big one; there is always an effective solution. I have learned to be patient with myself, and I no longer expect the perfection I demanded before I lost my sight.

I avoid negative thoughts that can send me spiraling down into depression and despair. It has not worked for me to try to exorcise my nighmares by painting them. The few times I have let myself put my fears on paper devastated me, and I fled the studio in search of distraction. It is not the terminal illness that will do me in. Life's small everyday hassles will eventually vanquish my spirit. If I succumb to the little voice of self-doubt, the big demons of my past and the monsters of my present will send me spiraling toward the end. This is why I paint concrete reality, rather than the hallucinogenic imaginings of my mind. It is why I paint bright, happy pictures. I have a favorite painting of a tiger. He is vital and content, surrounded by a field of orchids. In the zoo where I was allowed to pet him, he was sick and mangy and losing his teeth. I depicted him well fed and loved and set him in a perfect world.

I have numerous strategies for making myself laugh. Laughter is better than two aspirin, and a good comedy can carry me for two weeks. When I need a good belly laugh, I'll picture myself in a ludicrous situation—coming out of the shower to encounter a horrified guest who can't find the dining room, or the time I hugged the wrong guy at Foley's. In the midst of a crisis, I may not be able to conjure a full-on guffaw, but I can always manage a wan smile.

The relationship of my body to this rare condition is that of the cobra and the snake charmer. The chemotherapy and prednisone I take are the snake charmer, the cobra is the disease, and my body is the basket in which it resides. I do not, as the medical community frequently advises, "battle" my disease. It's a battle I cannot win. You can neither battle nor embrace a chronic condition. I think the best stance is one of détente. I accept it. I adjust to its ever-changing demands. I try to relax and let it be. Every action I undertake is based on a decision to maximize the moment while retaining balance.

It took a long, long time for me to stop obsessing about my disease. My vasculitis is tenacious and unpredictable in its effects; it is not going to disappear. I try to "notice" what's happening, but I avoid jumping to conclusions. I live with chronic low-grade pain that Tylenol won't touch. I do not take pills to dull the pain, and I have severe allergies to alcohol and narcotics. The pain is embedded in my operating system; it's just part of who I am. When I realized last year that my disease was more painful for Al than for me, I decided to stop talking about its physical effects.

Control is a seductive delusion. No matter how vigilant Al and I are, risk or no risk, rest or no rest, my health continues to decline. I might eat the same meal today as I did yesterday and end up as a 911 call, speeding toward the hospital, not knowing if I'll return home. I adhere to a very strict diet, because I am at risk for severe anaphylactic reactions to a number of foods and their derivatives. But I take great pleasure in a meal at a restaurant or a friend's house, so I'll venture out and enjoy myself, vigilantly, then return home to my plain yogurt and Perrier. With all the rabbit food and organic yogurt I eat, I should be a tall, svelte blonde. But it's not working; for some reason I remain a short, plump brunette.

The new me did not dwell for long on the Wentworth mess. Breaking the contract with the Wentworth Gallery was a crucial statement of self-direction. Finally—I meant it this time—I felt up to steering my own course, artistically and emotionally. Jason called and told me not to fret, reminding me that I was "destined to be a painter." I was developing my personal style, as well as my own personal therapy, in painting. I did forty oil paintings over the next year and sold every one of them. I was not a blind artist; I was an artist who happened to be blind. I did not require a gallery or a publisher, it seemed, just patrons who loved my work.

There is a kinship between the painter and the collector that touches both parties, even though they may never meet. I have sold over five hundred original paintings, so I feel like I've touched over five hundred lives. Thousands of people own my prints. For a solitary individual not given to friendship, this—not the fact that I paint—is a miracle. I enjoy commissioned work and the challenge of fulfilling the buyers' expectations. I feel that there is a specific painting or set of paintings for every buyer. It takes careful analysis to change a design, a subject, a color palette to custom-tailor the finished product, and I find the process intellectually stimulating. I like to think that each collector is getting something truly individual and unique. I like knowing that the owner can see what was on my mind, that my artistic thoughts and ideas as I worked on the canvas belong to him or her alone. For me, validation comes with knowing that my painting is on a sighted person's wall.

Painting is a form of communication, and the great masters have left their legacy of form, color, and beauty. I too hope to leave a legacy. But my art is still evolving. I am consumed with the logistics of painting, with the technical as well as the creative aspects. With the passage of time, I make progress toward a level of mastery that renders the technical aspects automatic, in my quest to create paintings special enough to survive me.

My excruciating love/hate relationship with painting is finally over. Today I unequivocally love painting. It's my lifeline and passion. Now I have a love/hate relationship with oils. Oil is the medium for me—I thank the Wentworth for that—but I still struggle with it daily. When you cannot see the canvas, oil painting is like navigating the Artic Circle without a map, dressed in a bikini with an elephant strapped to your back.

I like the fact that oil painting permits me to develop more complicated ideas. But the long drying time and the layered buildup of color demand time and patience. The more complicated the composition, the more difficult it is to retain a fixed image. The beauty is that you can set the painting aside while you rest and think about the composition, then return later and rework the dissatisfying parts. I'm becoming proficient at "fixing" my mistakes, just as I've become proficient at rescuing myself when I get into trouble. With oils, I can spread the pigment as thin as I want, building up the image in layers, glazing one thin layer of color over another. The slow-drying paint permits me flexibility, though I get frustrated with waiting for a "skin" to build up on the new layer so that I can work over it. I usually have several paintings at various stages of completion going at once. Since each canvas can be in a different stage of completion, I am never bored.

I like having the freedom to choose any size canvas, whereas watercolor is restricted by the limitations of available paper sizes. What I don't like is that I must stand up to paint. Unlike watercolor, with oil I can mount the canvas in any direction without worrying about the paint running. Often I turn the canvas upside down or sideways as I work, which enhances the energy of the painting.

The smell of turpentine, the toxicity, and the cleanup are definitely negatives. The studio must be kept immaculately clean. Everything must be scrupulously ordered, the paints lined up by color, everything in its proper place. (Al periodically checks to be sure that the paint tubes haven't gotten shuffled around.)

Washing oil brushes and work surfaces without sight is an ardu-ous and complicated process. But it's critical that I avoid touch-ing the paints and solvents, and that I prevent stains and odors from traveling throughout the studio. Sloppy cleanup tech-niques can be easily transferred onto the canvas. Maintaining a pristine work space is a serious problem for a born slob.

Because I cannot distinguish one color from another in oils, I find I must focus intensely. I must stay "in the zone" to keep track of the colors I am creating, and I have to hold on to the mental image evolving on the canvas. I cannot paint if I'm dis-tracted in any way. If I'm interrupted—by the telephone, an employee, a guest, Al—I have to lay out fresh paints on my rec-tangular palette. I can recall the image but not always the cur-rent layout of paint colors. I hate the waste.

I cannot judge the outcome of oils by feel, as I could with watercolor, so I am never certain that the perspective is correct, that the painting is finished, or that the final attempt works. I have to trust that my mind is linked to my brush, reliably con-verting my thoughts into the intended image. I am a little unnerved that I have yet to learn to paint the color of skin. Don't ask me how I know; I just do.

I'm dismayed by what I perceive as the primitive outcome of my paintings, and I continually struggle to master a more sophisticated image. Once I have learned what I need to know from a painting (with every painting my aim is to teach myself something new), it begins to bore me before it is actually done. On the other hand, often a subject doesn't get totally explored before the painting is sold. To me, this represents an uncom-pleted work. I have become proficient enough to replicate a piece, but I choose not to. Replication does not hasten my learning curve, since I cannot visually compare a sequence of paintings. *I like, I don't like*: you get the picture. Perhaps the need to have a love/hate conflict brewing in my life is my way of using stress productively. Or maybe I'm just ornery.

———————————

Today I went to answer the telephone, but when I picked up the receiver I could not hear the voice on the other end, the voices in the room, the sounds of the fan, or the clanking of kitchen utensils. When this happens, as it does more frequently these days, it can throw me for a loop, making me sick to my stomach and reawakening the terror I felt when my sight began to fail.

I was beyond terrified when I found out I was losing my hearing. It began with momentary lapses. I'd turn on the radio and . . . dead silence. Someone would be talking to me, and a phrase would drop out here and there. The prospect of deafness was so scary that I regressed to my old denial mode, just as I'd done when my vision problems began. I put off seeing the doctor, thinking that it would just go away. Al and I went on vacation. I hoped to leave my hearing loss in Las Vegas, but it followed me home. I confessed to Al that I was having hearing lapses.

"You are going deaf," the doctor reported when I finally went in for tests. "You already have a forty percent loss."

I didn't tell anyone except Claudia. I couldn't face the truth. "I can't see, and soon I won't be able to hear. How can I handle this, how can I respond to this?" I railed. "I feel like I'm on a bullet train heading into a tunnel."

Miraculously, over the next several months the regimen of chemotherapy and steroids I'd begun in the wake of the Wentworth debacle seemed to have a beneficial effect on my hearing and my general health. There were fewer noise dropouts, and the intermittent static seemed to lessen. My asthma calmed down. I felt fine, better than I had for a long time. I wasn't tired, and my shoulders didn't ache. *I must be getting better*, I thought. I decided I didn't need that toxic chemotherapy. I convinced myself it was bad for me. *After all, it is poison.* So I stopped taking it, without telling a soul.

Of course, my symptoms flared up real fast. My doctor was puzzled by the rapid deterioration of my hearing, given the intensive treatment he'd prescribed.

"Well, it's a painful disease," I evaded.

"With all this chemotherapy, you shouldn't be having all this pain," he countered. "Maybe I should up your dosage." I was busted.

When you are faced every day with your own decline, it is hard to accept reality. This is why someone who has had open-heart surgery doesn't stay on their diet, why smokers ignore the dire statistics, why people with osteoporosis don't exercise. Avoiding bad news is human nature, and some of us have it worse than others. Here I was bragging to everyone that I had come to terms with my life, that I'd accepted my vasculitis and lived in the moment, blah blah blah. Who was I trying to fool?

I went back on my chemotherapy regimen, but I had blown it. Once hearing function is lost, you don't recover it. The doctor gave me a stern lecture. "It's your choice, Lisa. If you don't stick to your regimen, you'll be dead in six months. No ifs, ands, or buts. Your otic nerve is already damaged; you are vulnerable to ministrokes." In other words, chemotherapy and discipline, or death.

What was I thinking? Well, what I was thinking was: I don't want to be a sick person who has to take chemotherapy. *I want to be healthy and normal for once.* It felt so good to feel asymptomatic for a change. It's like not paying your bills and thinking no one will notice. I let down my guard, and the Dragon jumped me.

CHAPTER ELEVEN

THE MIND'S EYE, THE HEART'S EASE

*When it is dark enough you can see
the stars.*

— CHARLES A. BEARD

BETWEEN MY LIFE AS AN INNKEEPER and my shows and Web sites, my life has become very public. The Oprah Winfrey show came to interview me soon after the Beauregard House opened, raising my visibility to a new level, in a way that felt right to me. I was finally ready to accept my fame as a blind artist. Whenever my "Remember Your Spirit" segment is rebroadcast in syndication, I get hundreds of e-mails. In 2002 a company called Motivational Productions highlighted my story in the annual feature-length film that it produces and distributes to schools all over the country. The subject that year was positive and negative boundaries—those we set for ourselves, as well as those imposed by fixed limitations, by our society, or by our misguided thinking. The film premiered at the Empire Theater here in San Antonio. At the opening, I felt like a star. I've gotten thousands of e-mails since this film was released, from educators and from kids telling me that my story helped them persevere and set boundaries for themselves, or encouraged them to stay in school.

People magazine's story on Al and me and our life at the Beauregard House brought more visibility. I've noticed recently that I'm a subject for speculation on numerous Internet forums and chat rooms. Check out chat rooms on sites like www.wetcanvas.com, www.getty.edu, www.artsed.net, and www.viscotland.org.uk, and you'll find people talking about the fascinating blind artist. I've come across discussions about me on sites in Europe, India, and Egypt.

It seems that many chat room participants have strong opinions about me as well as my artwork. The consensus seems to be that they like the art but are mystified by the artist. "Why would someone blind want to paint?" "Why doesn't she play the piano or throw pots? Beats me." "How does she keep her paints organized?" "What's with the figurative stuff?" Actually, my whole life seems to be a topic of analysis. "Why is she running a bed-and-breakfast?" "I hear she practices yoga."

Al used to read all the e-mail directed to me, but now I receive so much mail that he scans the postings and reads them to me only if they are funny or insightful. Until recently I would have been offended by all the attention, especially when, as is often the case, the opinions are critical and dismissive. "Her color sense has become distorted"; "The backgrounds are too complicated." Every negative review, every show rejection used to throw me into a tizzy. But I'm not so easily offended anymore. Criticism has become an important tool for improving my artwork. I can listen to what is said about me—believe me, some of it is pretty insulting—without getting bent out of shape. Telling myself that I am seeking a critique prepares me for the response. I'm finding that incorporating useful feedback is essential to improving my work.

Now that I accept myself, I don't desperately need the acceptance and approval of others. I enjoy the controversy, and I am happy that my work is considered significant enough to generate interest. I've gotten over the freak factor and realize that my life is motivational for others.

Occasionally I go online and involve myself with the discussions, especially when I can offer useful information or insight firsthand. Some of the commentary is flattering, even awestruck, and for the first time I'm able to accept it gracefully. My childhood fear that calling attention to myself and my accomplishments will explode in my face has faded, but I suppose my vacillation will never completely disappear. I will always be reminded about how different I was—too intelligent, too analytical, too introspective, too intense. It's only in recent years that I realize that the unnatural "oddball" qualities my parents hated about me are the very attributes that helped me survive.

I actively seek Jason's evaluation of my work, and he is always astute and helpful. I don't let him get away with "I like it" or "This doesn't work." I insist that he provide a full critique. We have an agreement that if paintings I've consigned to him are not sold after a specified time, I can reclaim them and rework them, or paint over them. Since entering into this agreement with Jason, I've never had to exercise this option. But having that trap door is mentally comforting.

My day-to-day life is pretty intense. On a typical day Al wakes me around seven A.M. Usually I exercise for half an hour, then join Al in the kitchen to help out while he prepares breakfast. This is our time to talk about our schedule and what needs to be handled that day. Al and I try to share the responsibilities of running the inn. I keep the books, pay the bills, and track the reservations. When I've had a bad night, I sleep in, and Al takes over the day's responsibilities. If I don't get eight hours of sleep, my circadian rhythm goes completely haywire, and I have a harder time than usual telling night from day. In my world, it's always nighttime. When I'm overtired, I don't like having to force myself to stay awake on sighted people's time.

My daily strategy, as Al puts it, is to "retreat, regroup, and return." Meaning that my way of coping with overload is to withdraw from my normal routine, replenish my energy, and then resume my active life. If I'm not up to painting, I'll drag one of my girlfriends along to go shopping for painting supplies. Sometimes just listening to a favorite CD helps me regroup. I'll go to a yoga class or join a bridge game. Bridge is a favorite new distraction, and it's great mental exercise. The cards have raised markings, so bidding is no problem, and each player calls out the card as it is played. Of course my memory is a big asset here.

How else do I amuse myself? I've been devoting time to learning Spanish. I listen to language tapes and practice my skills at every opportunity. I love to wander the neighborhood with Wizard, who, I'm sorry to say, is a flop as a guide dog. Travel never fails to give me an infusion of inspiration. In the past few years, we have been to Scotland, France, and Mexico, atmospheric places that nourish the mind's eye. Sometimes we just go to a beach condo on nearby South Padre Island and don't leave our room for a week. Sleep and sex, my favorite vacation recipe. Well, maybe we build one sand castle.

Somehow, despite the roller coaster of happiness and sadness, doubts and resistance, my life has come together. Cell by cell, a new person has replaced the woman whose world disappeared as she drove to work that fateful day on Interstate 35. Slowly, haltingly, I have come to a place where blindness is an integral part of my persona, and not some dreaded and unwanted intruder. Recently I caught myself saying, "I can't even remember what it is like not to be blind."

A group of professional women who stayed here recently asked me about my artistic goals. I told them that I had come to think of art as a *possibility* and not a goal. It has been a liberating experience to reach the stage where I am capable enough to be paid for my end product but lucky enough not to be able to judge it. No self-recrimination, no constant reexamination, just the contribution of the painting to someone's wall or life. "It's one of the things I love about being blind," I commented.

They were all over me in a second. "There are things you love about being blind?"

I had never really thought in those terms, but here I'd gone and blurted it out. So I had to acknowledge that yes, there were things about being blind that I'd come to appreciate. They didn't let me stop there. "Okay, let's have a list. What do you love about being blind?"

Here is what ended up on my list:

What I love about being blind is that I need only one pencil. Al probably has a hundred pencils in his office because he never puts them back. I have one pencil, because I always put it back in the same place, so I always know where it is.

Another plus is that I've become an expert at reading people's voices. Voices tell the real story. To me, voices are more revealing than body language. I can spot hypocrisy, enthusiasm, conflict, aloofness, warmth, frustration, and annoyance in the voice of any person who enters my life. It is not possible for me to be thrown off the scent by visual information like tense shoulders or a false smile. Yogi Berra said, "You can observe a lot just by watching." I "watch" the tone of voice.

What I love about being blind is that I am no longer a consumer—and I used to be a world-class consumer. I've lost the desire for many things I used to think were necessary. Shopping with my friends, hearing them exclaim over their purchases, gives me great pleasure. Sometimes they'll insist that I buy a whimsical item, but Al chooses all my clothes and makeup.

What I love best is not worrying about how I look. I can feel the effects of aging creeping up on my face and hips, but without the reminder in the mirror, I will always be eighteen. My beauty is timeless!

Blindness makes me feel that I've paid my dues, so I'm free to reward myself. "You did good this week, you cleared up your e-mail backlog, you didn't blow your diet," I tell myself, "so you can have your nails done." In truth, I've gotten to the point where I'll get my nails done whether I've been good or not. Every time I am self-indulgent, I think of Mark Twain saying "eat what you like and let the food fight it out inside." I exempt myself from what Claudia calls "adult behavior," which really amounts to an overblown sense of guilt and responsibility. I know all about that. I used to believe that if I just did the right thing and didn't make waves, nothing terrible would happen to me.

What I most love is that blindness forced me to change. I'm a kinder, happier person, with a meaningful life. I have dear friends, a loving marriage, a passion for art. Crisis equals opportunity. Blindness opened up something in me that would have otherwise remained closed.

Having lost my sight, I figure nothing worse can happen to me. My ghastly childhood didn't destroy me, my miserable first marriage didn't consume me, blindness didn't eradicate me, so I guess deafness won't do me in. It's merely another journey into the unknown. In the years since I lost my sight, I've developed coping mechanisms and a basis of personal security that will help me weather any storm. I'm not sure that I could survive losing Al, but I have a better chance now than before. I can survive anything and be happy. Truly happy.

Quite a list, no? If you had told me five years ago that I'd be reciting a litany of the things I love about being blind, I would have thought you were nuts.

I have been very ill these past years. There's always something going on with my health, so we are always trying to stay a step ahead of the next crisis. By now, I've seen so many specialists I could start a referral service. Deafness beckons, another layer of darkness that threatens to cut me off from the world I've come to love. My sensorineural hearing loss is another consequence of the vasculitis that took my sight. The prognosis for my hearing is grim. The doctor has instructed me to call immediately if there is any sudden change in my hearing. "Do you understand that you need to contact me the *minute* there is a change," he stressed, remembering the precautionary lectures I'd ignored when I'd first started to lose my hearing.

At this point I can barely discriminate between an *f* and an *s,* a *d* and a *t,* or similar-sounding words like *ball* and *hall* and *call* and *tall.* I've given up trying to understand conversations in crowded rooms, for fear that I've misunderstood what's being discussed. We've purchased phones designed for the hearing impaired with handsets and volume controls that boost the sound. Even so, I find myself inadvertently cutting people off in midsentence. I abhor my unintentional rudeness, but I miss the interaction with people. I've learned to ask for patience, explaining that I am going deaf. I don't want to book a flight to Peru and wind up in Timbuktu, so I ask people to repeat themselves until I am certain I understand. This is a big step for someone who didn't admit she was blind for two years. Now I am paying close attention to the course of my hearing loss and taking measures to adapt.

My greatest worry is whether I will be able to continue painting. If I don't have the input of my hearing, which has become the most valuable source of imagery for my paintings, will I recall the pulse of the dance, the *olés* of the bullfight, the intimacy of conversation, the clamor of a street scene? Will I develop the ability to retain aural memories, as I do visual information? How will I file and retrieve aural data? If I can't paint, can I change my focus to sculpting? How will I keep my batteries charged?

All my fears need to be categorized and sorted into boxes for careful analysis, before the next phase begins. Which fears are valid, and which are not? I need to know what can be done to handle each one, should it arise. I need to know that I can continue to paint and to function. As blindness erases the world, deafness erases the sense of community. I am counting on the fact that life, like art, endures.

More than ever, painting is my lifeline. On days when my energy flags, I paint in short, fifteen-minute stretches. I spend a lot of time snuggled in my big cozy chair, listening to music and communing with my paintings. I have begun to reflect more and paint less, which is creating stronger work.

Not that the old doubts don't creep in. Not that I don't still struggle to assure myself that my work is valid. But those times are few and far between. More and more I paint for myself—my own pleasure, my own entertainment, my own learning and intellectual challenge. My attention is focused on pure creativity and self-expression. Lately I've been trying to get a handle on painting water and reflection—without much success so far, but I'm having a good time trying. The more complicated a painting problem, the more I welcome it.

There is a connection that I don't fully understand between my diminishing hearing and the desire to tackle complex canvases. I'm completely bored with painting architecture, perhaps because I can neither see nor hear buildings. Almost every painting now involves multiple figures, in a detailed setting, with a complicated perspective. For years I told myself I wanted to paint a thousand people bathing on the shores of the Ganges River. I think this was partly my old "I'll show you" attitude. I may yet get to this painting, but for now half a dozen antiques dealers browsing in an auction house will suffice.

Some of my skills have noticeably improved. My ability to imagine detailed scenarios is stronger than ever. My private world of blindness is like a stereoscope that allows me to flip through an immense library of images. I take pains to confirm the accuracy of these images with others, but I also accept that my own distortions of "real" life are valid in themselves, simply an alternative perspective. My mental mapping skills have grown, and I no longer need to preplan my paintings in such painstaking detail. I can hold an image so well that I am able to paint a complex canvas without any preliminary drawing. Often I have several color palettes going at once, and I might use up the paints from all of them in the preliminary stages of a new canvas, without regard to hue, as a means of building up layers of complexity. My intention is to be a strong value painter rather than a colorist, which means that I concern myself primarily with compositional massing and unity. I find that if I get the primary masses correct, with clearly defined lights and darks, the details will follow.

The biggest change is that I can alter the drawing and placement of objects over time, as I work on the canvas, painting out what I no longer want and adding new elements. I can lose or gain an edge on a whim, or skew the design as I go. I have no clue as to how I am able to do this. More and more, my imagery seems to arise from some automatic source. I'm trying to incorporate some of the old masters' techniques I've studied, and I have even begun to experiment with techniques of my own that are the beginning indications of a personal style. Al says that I am making huge leaps in my skill level and development.

In short, I am becoming a real painter, not someone who sells paintings to prove her dollar value. I still get invited to lecture and conduct seminars and workshops, and I enjoy demonstrating what I have learned to the public. Shows of my work opened in recent years that I planned to attend, but the paintings sold out before the openings. My paintings turn up in movies and on book jackets, as magazine covers and posters. It pleases me that my work has such broad appeal. I continue to strive for mastery over art—and life, for that matter—but I recognize that contentment comes in the immersion process alone. I am an ordinary person, albeit blind, who is compelled to paint. When I recently mentioned this to Jason he said, "Well, Lisa, people may buy your paintings because they are intrigued by what you do, but I don't think anyone is paying thousands of dollars merely for the novelty of owning work by a blind painter. They are buying the work of Lisa Fittipaldi, artist."

———————

"Retreat, regroup, return" is not just my day-to-day modus operandi. It sums up my journey since I lost my sight. First I retreated: I withdrew from the world and refused to adapt to my situation. Then I regrouped: I learned the practical and spiritual skills I needed to live my life. And finally I returned to the world, and to a fuller, more authentic version of myself.

I would not trade a moment of the years since losing my sight to return to my old life. Sight is not a fair swap for being alone, without intimate friendships and my precious marriage. I am not jealous of anyone else's life, as I am too busy relishing my own. I lost my sight, but I gained clarity of vision. The little voice that once told me I was not worthy is dead. One day, I realized that I'd made it well into my fifties without having lost anything more than my vision and my health. I was still breathing, and I could put on my underwear correctly. The nagging voice faded and disappeared. Just how I arrived at this spot is a mystery, but I can look back over the road I've traveled for clues. One thing I know for sure: happiness is not the goal; it is the means of transportation.

I will soon to fly off to Oaxaca, Mexico, on my own for an intensive Spanish course. It is my first solo vacation. This trip is a statement to myself that I am still alive and in the world. It is a challenge to my independence, another notch in the yardstick of my life. I am both scared and excited. I don't know how I'll fare without the safety net of Al or a friend. I wonder if I can handle the hearing blackouts, the unknown terrain, and the unfamiliar culture. Will the food or water make me ill? The memory of my air-travel fiascos haunts me. I am afraid of regressing into depression and dependence.

I want my two weeks in Oaxaca to reassure me of my strengths and enlighten me as to my weaknesses. My hope is that the time away will give me the opportunity to integrate and adapt, and to have an adventure on my own. When I come back, I will know just where I came from and where I am going. For me, *travel* is a means of happiness. I'll retreat to Oaxaca. I'll regroup my energies. And then I'll return home.